Using Talk Effectively in the Primary Classroom

Richard Eke and John Lee

Routledge
Taylor & Francis Group

LONDON AND NEW YORK

First published 2009 by Routledge
2 Park Square, Milton Park, Abingdon, Oxon, OX14 4RN

Simultaneously published in the USA and Canada
by Routledge
170 Madison Ave, New York, NY 10016

Routledge is an imprint of the Taylor & Francis Group, an informa business

© 2009 Richard Eke and John Lee

Typeset in Galliard by Pindar New Zealand
Printed and bound in Great Britain by
CPI Antony Rowe, Chippenham, Wiltshire

British Library Cataloguing in Publication Data
A catalogue record for this book is available from the British Library

Library of Congress Cataloging-in-Publication Data
Eke, Richard.
  Using talk effectively in the primary classroom / Richard Eke and John Lee.
    p. cm.
  1. Children—Language. 2. Oral communication. 3. Language arts (Primary)
  I. Lee, John. II. Title.
  LB1139.L3E413 2008
  372.1102′2—dc22   2008009460

ISBN 10: 0-415-34281-3 (pbk)
ISBN 13: 978-0-415-34281-0 (pbk)

Contents

Illustrations

Figures

Tables

Acknowledgements

We thank the schools, pupils and teachers we worked with for their help and willingness to be observed and recorded. Without their co-operation this book would not have been possible.

Our colleagues Gordon Guest, Nick Clough, Yvonne Davies and Martin Ashley (now at Edge Hill University) provided data and examples for chapters on science, information and communication technology (ICT) and religious education, and we thank them.

Any book of this kind is the result of discussions both in our Faculty and outside of it. We are sure that we have drawn on the ideas and insights of our colleagues but of course any errors are our own.

We have been fortunate in our analysis of classroom data, both here and in other places, to have been able to exploit the flexibility of the software 'Merlin' and have appreciated dialogue with Keith Hughes on its usage.

Pam Flew has patiently dealt with what was sometimes a mangled text and Lynn Goh was always on hand to provide help and refreshment.

Finally we would like to thank Bruce Roberts for his comments on the various iterations of our text.

Introduction

This book is about talk in primary school classrooms, but we will not let this prohibit us from drawing on examples from pre-school years where they will help us to clarify how talk does and can work. We focus particularly on the language teachers use in their teaching but we always link this with the ways in which their pupils talk and, most important, the ways in which talking becomes learning. We put it in this rather clumsy way because teachers use language all the time, not just when they are teaching. So you will not find any focus in this book on the language teachers use when they discipline children or the language they use when talking to colleagues, headteachers or parents. It is an optimistic book for two principal reasons. First, we believe that by studying the language use of skilled teachers in challenging situations we can help other teachers to become more effective. Second, the book seeks to relate teaching to learning and learning to teaching, so that we always keep in mind the role of the learner as well as the role of the teacher.

There are many interesting and instructive texts which seek to advise on the most effective teaching methods. These texts almost always adopt a view that there is clear evidence that doing something in one particular way will always produce predictable and desirable outcomes. We have been careful not to take a position like this. We have used data and their analysis to produce evidence of how teachers and their pupils can become better and more effective talkers for learning. In brief, we do not have the kind of model of the effective teacher that you will find in the literature on school effectivity and school improvement. Our approach has been to analyse in detail the classroom talk of sophisticated and skilful teachers. We then go on to ask what lessons we can learn from these teachers and their classrooms.

There is considerable literature on classroom language. Britton (1967) argued that there was a critical relationship between language and learning and in making that argument he prioritised an understanding of language in use in the classroom as critical. He stressed the importance of talk in the lives of children.

> Talk is a major instrument in learning in infancy, that the infant *learns by talking* and that he *learns to talk by talking*. (Ibid.: 129)

Britton goes on to argue that learning by talking is crucial in all schooling. Following Britton, the most optimistic writers have tried to show what kind of language is more likely to support learning. Douglas Barnes, in his pioneering work, talked of open-ended questions – the sorts of questions that enabled pupils to put forward their own ideas. Barnes may be taken as representative of a view of language use in classrooms and how it relates to learning, albeit that his focus was secondary school classrooms. Barnes (1977), Barnes et al. (1986) and others of the same persuasion – Rosen (1971), Britton (1967) and those teachers involved in the London Association for the Teaching of English – went beyond focusing on the teacher and argued that the best language use came about when pupils were enabled to talk to each other in small groups without the supervision of a teacher. Let us just remind ourselves that this work was conducted in secondary schools and most often during English lessons. While this pioneering work offered general descriptions of language use, our work offers a detailed framework for description and analysis that enables us to be far more specific about language use, so we have gone beyond terms such as 'open questions'. Having said that, without the pioneering work of these authors and their colleague school teachers, our work would have lacked inspiration.

Following on from these pioneers, we would argue that there is now a well-established body of scholarship dedicated to language use in classrooms. As this work evolved, clear links were established with work on pedagogy. Brian Simon had noted in the early 1980s how little work there was on the nature of pedagogy in England and we will return to his view later. However, since the middle 1980s there has been a focus on pedagogy in primary schools, although these scholars defined 'pedagogy' somewhat differently from Simon. A government-commissioned report authored by Alexander, Rose and Woodhead (1992) initiated a debate about primary school pedagogy; up to that point, official documents had eschewed any pedagogical advice or prescription, leaving the way the National Curriculum was to be taught to teachers and schools. Although in parts its tone was strident, it was bold in making clear recommendations as to what classroom practice should look like. The recommendations amounted to urging primary teachers to teach subjects and to engage in much more whole class teaching and much less group work. The advent of the *Literacy Strategy* as a national initiative in 1997 marks a further move towards a prescriptive pedagogy and the enshrining of whole class teaching as the most effective way to teach. In our chapter on literacy teaching (Chapter 5), we offer some analysis and commentary on teaching during what was then called the 'literacy hour'. One year after the establishment of the *National Literacy Strategy*, the *National Numeracy Strategy* came into play in primary classrooms; as with the teaching of literacy, we offer commentary and analysis of numeracy in classrooms.

We have collected data on skilled teachers teaching literacy, numeracy, ICT, science and religious education. In each of these instances we have focused on the way teachers teach. Each of the teachers we studied was working in a challenging situation. Some of the teachers were working in rural schools with mixed age groups and having to plan and implement learning outcomes appropriate to the different chronological ages in the classroom. Some of the teachers were working in inner city schools with very high percentages of socially disadvantaged pupils and high percentages of pupils deemed to have special educational needs. We try to show how we can learn from these teachers in order to improve our own classroom performance.

Robin Alexander has produced a succession of publications describing and defining what primary classroom pedagogy should or might look like. In his 1992 book *Policy and Practice in Primary Education*, he effectively established the field that he would cover since then. He has argued that primary school teachers need to be confident in the knowledge they are teaching and should have a clear view of how effective teaching should proceed. In the case of language use, drawing on the work of Bakhtin, he has argued that good quality teaching should be 'dialogic'. While we have used the term 'discursive', we have also tried to show that the voices of learners need to be enabled by a teaching method that encourages them to express their views, ideas and feelings.

When we gathered the evidence of good practice used in the book, this merging of the *National Literacy Strategy* and *National Numeracy Strategy* into the *Primary National Strategy* had not occurred. We therefore make reference both to the individual strategies and to the current national strategy. When we refer to the two separate strategies, we often use the acronyms NLS (*National Literacy Strategy*) and NNS (*National Numeracy Strategy*). In the case of religious education and ICT, we have drawn on materials published by the Qualifications and Curriculum Authority (QCA) and the Department for Education and Skills (DfES), now Department for Children, Schools and Families (DfCSF).

The book is in two parts: the first part sets out our general argument and describes the mode of description and analysis we use; the second part offers examples of classroom practice and tries to show what lessons we might learn. Overall we have argued that teachers need to be able to reflect on their practice in an analytic manner and to conduct a fine-grained analysis of their language use. Since we are in an era in which whole class teaching has become very much the norm, we have focused on that, but in doing so do not mean to suggest that there is no place for group work. We have indicated in our account of science how well-organised group work enhances learning. In the future, as primary teachers are joined by more learning support assistants (LSAs), group work will be easier to support but will only be effective if teachers can make the language use of learning supporters cognitively orientated. In the book we use methods enabling us to analyse classroom talk. We know that if adults talk to children in particular ways, this helps children to talk in ways that empower them to learn more effectively. In order to develop an analytic approach to these aspects of teaching, you can use the methods and models we present for you. As you read the book we will remind you of this.

An important feature of the book is our use of suggested activities. You will find these in all chapters. You can conduct many of them on your own or in collaboration with your colleagues. Others specifically ask you to collaborate. The activities are of different kinds. Some ask you to undertake empirical enquiries in your own classroom; these offer you advice and guidance on how to conduct such research. Others ask you to reflect on research and commentary and ask what lessons you might learn from that. Sometimes this is a large slice of actual classroom talk collected by different researchers. At the end of each chapter, you will find a short section on lesson learning but, remember, you will learn in your own way and may learn different lessons because you have further developed as a reflective practitioner.

Finally you will notice that we have used the words 'pupil' and 'pupils' throughout. We could have used the word 'children' but prefer the words 'pupil' and 'pupils' because they make clear that we are talking about teaching and learning in a formal school setting. In brief, we argue that children are always children but once they enter school they learn how to become pupils and, once they have that role, they stand in a special relationship to teachers and supporters.

Part One

In this part of the book we discuss the importance of talk and how you can describe what is going on in classrooms, including your own classroom. It is easy to make statements such as 'talking and listening are very important'. The challenge is to show what kinds of speaking and listening are better ways to ensure pupils' learning. We need to be able to argue the case for talking against a tradition of trying to make the children silent in classrooms. There is also a strong tradition that only values pupil talk when it is a direct response to a teacher's question of fact. The challenge we face is both how to get pupils to use talk and how we can view it as valuable and valued. In brief, how we can identify when talking is learning in the formal sense.

In the closing years of the last century and at the beginning of this one, teaching from the 'front' has been eulogised. Alexander, Rose and Woodhead (1992) and Reynolds and Farrell (1996) made strong cases for a type of whole class teaching that prioritised the role of the teacher as the only transmitter of knowledge and skills. A range of researchers have examined these views and you will find reference to them later in the book. It is our view that recognising the importance of whole class teaching does not mean accepting one viewpoint nor does it exclude the use of children's own ideas in lessons. We want to argue that whole class teaching is better when we have a more sophisticated idea of how talking and learning relate to each other and how skilled teachers are able to focus attention on learning in its broadest sense. This matches the professional standards for England which state that, in order to qualify as a teacher, student teachers must evaluate the impact of their teaching on the progress of all learners. This means being able to identify pupils' cultural, linguistic and emotional development.

The book discusses children's linguistic, social and cultural development, but we focus here specifically on the linguistic and – just as important – how we can describe what talk is like in classrooms. In the chapters in this part we draw attention to how we can 'take account of, and support pupils' varying needs so that girls and boys from all ethnic groups can make good progress' (TDA 2002). In the context of whole class teaching, we argue that it is very important to be able to analyse what is happening in classrooms so that we can learn lessons from good practice. So we begin by looking at some of the research that has examined what happens in classrooms. We do not claim to review everything, only that work relevant to our own way of working. We will show in each chapter how research conducted by others relates to what we are proposing and indicate how you can use it yourself.

In this part, you will meet material that will enable you to meet the relevant Training and Development Agency (hereafter TDA) standards for initial teacher training and professional development. These standards demand that those in training learn how to reflect on and improve their practice and, after qualification, be able to improve practice through professional development. Advanced skills teachers are required to be able to research and evaluate curriculum practices and the research reviewed in this part will help in doing this. The chapters will also contribute to your understanding of the way that pupils' learning relates to their linguistic development and to your understanding of the importance of language in classroom planning.

In order to research your own practice and the curriculum, you need to develop research skills. First, you need to know about methods that are relevant to and usable by the practitioner. There are a number of methods you will already be familiar with – perhaps the most prominent is 'action research' – but what we offer in this book is a way of getting at the fine detail of classroom talk. In this part, you will find references and commentary on a range of research methods alongside the ones we have used. We hope that by the time you have read Part One, you will appreciate the ways that talk has been researched and the possibilities of your embarking on your own reflective research aimed at improving the quality of talking and learning in your class and your school.

So in the first chapter, you will find accounts of research that shows what children can do with talk before they come to school. It also asks you to look carefully at some data and think about what they tell you. Other research introduced here shows how some children come to school, as it were, equipped with 'school language'. In the second chapter you will find how school talk might be commented on and how it is very different from ordinary language. The third chapter introduces you to some research and research methods that have shown us what life in primary classrooms is like if looked at via talk. Here you will find activities asking you to consider 'teacher talk'. In the final chapter of this part, we continue to explore classroom interaction with a look at 'scaffolding'. It is in this chapter, as we explore what scaffolding means, that we set out in detail our methodology and mode of analysis.

Chapter 1

The talk accomplishments of children starting primary school

Children are always children, but they have to learn to be pupils. Before they become pupils they can do many things, so before looking at classrooms let's see what children can do with talk and what schools do with it.

In this chapter, we introduce you to the following ideas:

- Nearly all children come to school as effective talkers.
- They use talk to make meaning.
- The making of meaning is a social activity.
- School knowledge is different.
- School talk is 'strange' and specific to school.
- For some children, there is a gap between talking for meaning and talking for school.
- The way teachers talk to children can change the size of this gap.
- The work of Basil Bernstein and some of his critics is relevant.

In this chapter you will find something about how children develop language, and how they use talk to develop their thoughts. You will also find some reference to the way that Basil Bernstein describes school knowledge as being encoded in a kind of 'school language' which is different from everyday language.

Let's look at some of the evidence that shows what children can do with talk before and just as they enter school. Children come to school as thinkers because they use language to make meaning, communicate meaning and symbolise their experiences. The psychologist Vygotsky argues that language and thought are inextricably linked and that all children, by using language in social settings, become thinkers. He believes that as children's thought develops in more and different ways, they need more differentiated forms of talk.

The evidence collected by linguists, language development researchers and educationalists interested in the very early years all indicates that children enter formal schooling with the accomplishment of skilled language users. This is true even in England, where children generally begin formal schooling as early as four or four-and-a-half years old.

What do we mean by 'accomplishment' here? Let's start by saying what we don't mean. We do not mean that all children come to school equipped to follow and join in with the talk conventions so often found in classrooms. In a later chapter we describe how strange and artificial classroom talk is in comparison to everyday talk.

Linguists interested in children's talk have shown that even comparatively young children are rather sophisticated users of language. They are able to use the grammar of the language to make themselves understood and are also able to use grammar creatively. More than this, they seem to have an understanding that grammar is a set of descriptive rules that can be drawn upon. For instance, although English-speaking four-year-olds often use the past tense of 'ran', they tend to generalise the grammatical rule and say 'runned'. So contrary to what some teachers believe, and believed in the past, children's linguists and language development scholars on the whole argue that children's language is not an inferior sort of adult talk but that it is a form of its own. We have used here a very well-known example of a four-year-old's use of a verb that we now know most of them have grasped and can use. Linguists such as Chomsky point to the 'error' of using 'runned' as evidence that the child knows and can use complex grammatical rules governing the nature of the verb.

Activity
'Dada allgone'
Make a list of possible meanings for this expression.

'Daddy allgone' is typically produced by children aged about eighteen months. When using the phrase 'Daddy allgone', a parent could attribute a range of possible meanings that will be linked to the context. The mother may confirm that daddy has gone to the shop or somewhere else if she treats it as a question. She may treat it as a statement and say 'that's right, he's not here'. Daddy may be being told that the child has finished their lunch or be being asked if they have finished it. We can note that it is at about two years of age that children produce utterances in which their meaning is clear from their talk.

How do you think the meanings and the talk are related?
What do you think the following mean?
Is it easy to define meaning without knowing the context?

Issy eat
Dada jump

Eat biccie
Johnny sock
Horse doggie
All gone
All broke
Poor teddy

Children's talk is a little different from adult talk in that it is almost always tied to particular situations. The richness of their developing language use seems to arise from their interaction with adults eager to understand the child's meaning. Michael Halliday (1975), in his study of language development, shows how children and adults combine to make sense of even the youngest child's approximations of talk. What seems to happen is that the meanings of a young child's sounds are established in the 'space between' the child and the adult. So the linguistic development of the child is part of their development as a social being; they do not develop language use by themselves. Here is a well-known example – when a child first produces the 'da da' sound, their mother may well say 'Daddy's not here'. Let's look at another example. 'Mummy gup' is an interesting phrase, if you think about it. It could mean that the child is pointing and saying 'That is mummy's cup'. Let's try another context for the same phrase, such as when the child holds out their hand and their words take on a new meaning – 'Mummy, can I have a cup?' In this kind of talk, the object referred to, the 'gup', is present; talk becomes even more sophisticated when the person or thing referred to is absent. This is really the beginning of the use of language to describe and convey ideas. In this case, the object is not physically present and cannot be pointed at.

As the child's language develops, we can see them experimenting with sounds and with a range of grammatical structures. What is also happening is that the child is learning to make meanings by interacting with an adult in a familiar context. Here is an example of an interaction between a child (C) and her mother (M):

C: (*Wearing a jacket and pointing to her neck.*) Up up.
M: What?
C: Neck up.
M: Neck? What do you want? What?
C: Neck.
M: What's on your neck?
C: (*Points to zipper and lifts her chin up.*) Zip zip zip. (Wells 1987)

What we can see here is how the child is struggling to make herself understood; the mother joins in by asking pertinent questions. This child is not merely learning to answer questions in order to be understood, she is also learning the nature of this kind of conversation, the rules of social conversation. When she has acquired these rules, she can use them herself to establish the meanings that others make. Many of you will have encountered the child who has mastered these particular rules and enjoys continuously asking 'Why?' questions.

McLure (1992), using 'snippets of chat' which are not particularly remarkable, demonstrates how effective and efficient the language use of five-year-olds is. She notes that, apart from a few children who have particular difficulties, five-year-olds do not merely have a large vocabulary and the ability to use the majority of adult grammar, but they are able to play with language and are already developing an awareness of the genres of adult talk. Five-year-olds are well able to tell jokes; the jokes they tell are usually dependent on a sophisticated understanding of lexical and or structural ambiguity. Try these examples of lexical ambiguity, for instance:

> What do you call a cow who munches on your lawn?
> A lawnmooer.

> What has four wheels and flies?
> A rubbish lorry.

This kind of linguistic playfulness is the commonest that children use. But they can also appreciate structural ambiguity, and we know this because they tell and laugh at jokes like this:

> Girl: Last night I opened the door in my nightie.
> Boy: That's a funny place to keep a door.

In this case, the joke depends on whether 'in' modifies 'door' or 'nightie'. You have to be a sophisticated user of the language, with an understanding of the rules of grammar, to laugh at this joke; children do laugh. Both kinds of jokes challenge verbal and conversational conventions. This indicates that children ought not to have trouble with the language of schooling, but some appear to have such trouble. So you will, perhaps, already be thinking that not all children come to school with the kind of cultural capital that enables them easily to engage with formal school knowledge. The puzzle is why these adept language users often become monosyllabic and even mute after a relatively short experience of formal schooling.

All of this language learning has been accomplished, by children, in a context where their meanings have been prioritised. Schools necessarily are unable to prioritise the meaning of every individual child, because it is the job of schools to transmit formal knowledge – that is, in the case of English primary schools, knowledge about arithmetic, reading, writing, art, history etc. There is also pressure on schools and teachers to inculcate knowledge that can be tested and, because of this, schools may ignore what children actually know and treat them as though they had very little skill in language use. Unfortunately many adults, including some teachers, treat children as though they have a very restricted use of language.

What schools expect is that children easily move into language use that, while less creative, makes very different demands. Instead of being able to negotiate meaning and explore language with an adult in a familiar environment and in an individual manner, the child has to deal with a set of meanings that are determined already and do so as one of a crowd.

We have shown you that research – and probably your own experience – indicates that most children are very good communicators. What needs to be thought about now is the critical difference between home and school. School makes demands on children which home does not, although for some children the language demands of school are not so different from those they encounter at home. The sociologist Basil Bernstein refers to those children arriving equipped for school language as having a sort of 'cultural subsidy'. These children know you can have pink elephants in a maths activity or in a story but you can't have them in your news book.

School usually asks for reasons in a way that is different from everyday life. You may say to a friend that you are going out in the evening, and will probably say where you are going. What you would not expect is to have to give reasons for your choice of venue, or why this evening rather than any other. If you remember your own school days, you were almost always expected to give both kinds of reasons for your actions. Talk of this kind occurs in some homes but not in others, so some children are more familiar than others with such talk. It is usually referred to as 'universal', in that the reasons are not necessarily dependent on the specific circumstance. So, to return to the example, you might say that you are going out because it enhances your well-being or you might say that you got a free ticket. The first is context free, while the second is not so, and is usually referred to as being 'context bound'. Saying that you have a free ticket only offers a reason if the hearer knows the context. Let's say it is a free ticket to the ballet or a club, and clearly you'd only use it if you liked the activity and your hearer would know that if they knew the context. In other words, at least part of the meaning is implicit.

Activity

Which of these utterances are 'context bound', with their meaning being tied to the specific context and particular to that circumstance? Which are relatively 'context free', with their meaning being derived directly from the language and covering a variety of possible circumstances? This latter kind of language use yields meanings that are called 'universal' rather than 'specific' or 'particular'.

He kicked the ball and it went through that window.
The window was broken by accident because he mis-kicked the ball.

Two plus two.

Up up up. (Printed below a picture of a boy holding a toy aeroplane and pointing its nose upwards.)

I told you to shut up.

Sit down because we are going to watch the television.

Some of the language in the activity above illustrates that what children are able to learn in school can be very limited by the way in which schools rely on the universal for talking about important matters. Can you think of some examples of your own?

We are saying that only being able to understand the particular context is very limiting for children. It is a fact that some children come to school better equipped to deal with the universal, but this does not mean that the other children have some kind of linguistic deficit. What we can say is that the well-equipped rapidly and readily become pupils and, as you can appreciate, this has powerful consequences for the rest of their school lives.

The important idea that school knowledge is encoded in such a way that it requires universal meanings comes from the work of Basil Bernstein. To put this rather too simply, the fact of a child's not being an everyday user of a linguistic and cultural code that carries universal meaning blocks that child's unlimited potential for learning. Bernstein calls this the 'elaborated code' and the context-bound use as the 'restricted code'.

Young (2002) says:

> The two types of language code are the restricted code and the elaborated code. Now, to avoid misunderstanding, it is noted that the restricted code does not refer to restricted vocabulary just as elaborated code does not refer to better, more eloquent language.

Young goes on to say:

> The restricted code works better than the elaborated code for situations in which there is a great deal of shared and taken-for-granted knowledge in the group of speakers.

So Bernstein is not talking about the use of Standard English; he is talking about the way meanings are made and encoded. Most schools operate in a version of Standard English and so an unfortunate confusion has arisen and many people think that the use of Standard English is the same as the use of the elaborated code. Children come to school speaking the language of home, which may or may not have given them extensive experience of the sort of language codes that school uses.

Basil Bernstein argues that formal school knowledge is encoded in a specific way – something he originally referred to as an elaborated code but which, as we said above, is not simply a matter of language. Indeed, it is about the transmission of knowledge. Basil Bernstein argues that knowledge is unequally distributed and that this inequity is partly maintained by the code of transmission. We could put this rather starkly, in a society organised around social class, affirming that working-class pupils, on the whole, will have access to a more limited range of knowledge than their middle-class peers.

When children first enter school, they encounter some rather strange examples of language use. Initially these are often associated with classroom rules of behaviour. Basil Bernstein calls this the 'regulatory discourse' and notes that it goes hand in hand with what he calls the 'instructional discourse'. The latter focuses on knowledge, what children are expected to learn, often for the purposes of tests. So managing the children becomes bound up with teaching them. There is an element of common sense in this, as teachers are expected to teach the children and, in order to do this, they need the children to listen and attend; in other words, formal schooling requires the children to comply with what the teacher wants them to do. There is little opportunity for the children to choose an activity, and none when the teaching involves whole class instruction. It is too easy forget how the social arrangements of school seem to produce the strange and artificial talk associated with these arrangements. Here are some examples of the strangeness of the regulatory discourse.

'Let us all sit on the carpet, please.'

This looks like a polite invitation. Invitations by their nature may be refused, however you know that there are penalties for refusing if you are a Reception class child. It is not an invitation; it is a command.

'Would you like to tidy the bookshelf?'

This also looks like an invitation. The use of the weak modal verb 'would' suggests the possibility of refusal. You might be asked 'Would you like another drink?' And you would feel very happy saying no. Of course, the child who refuses to tidy the bookshelf will find themselves in some trouble.

Both these examples demonstrate the strangeness of classroom language use and, as a consequence, the linguistic strangeness of the regulatory discourse.

Activity
Collect six examples of this sort of teacher talk and analyse them as we have done above. As an extension, you might compare the language use of classroom adult volunteers.

What do you make of this statement: 'I hope we are all doing our work.'

It is comparatively easy to see how statements of the kind above, however confusing, are intended to maintain an environment conducive to teaching and learning.

Schools regulate the actions of children in very precise ways. When was the last time you asked for permission to the leave a room? Take the case of using the lavatory; if you were visiting a strange house, in order to be polite you would probably seek permission, something like 'May I use your loo?' As you know this is really a request for directions, it's a polite way of asking 'Where is it?' You would be gobsmacked if your host replied, 'Certainly not. Why didn't you go before you came in?' or said, 'Ask me again in five minutes'.

Activity
Make a list of the activities that require children to ask the teacher's permission to do. Categorise them into those that would not require permission outside the classroom and those that would.

The language of regulation is indeed very strange, but we made it so by focusing on it and questioning below the surface. It is equally true to say that the language of school instruction, Bernstein's 'instructional discourse', is strange. The problem is that its very strangeness almost ensures the locking-out of good language users who make powerful use of the restricted code.

Just to make the point even more strongly about the effectiveness of young children's talk, have a look at these two famous extracts from a study of language development. The researchers tracked the language use of children and parents at home and then children and teachers in school (Wells 1987: 95–6).

Rosie is described as having slower development than other children in the sample. She comes from a large working-class family who were experiencing poverty at the time of the research. Here is Rosie (R) talking with her mother (M):

M: We got to make the beds later on.
R: Uh?
M: Make the beds.
R: Come on then.
M: Not yet.
R: What, in a minute?
M: Yeah, in a minute.
R: What time have we got to do it?
M: I don't know – I'll see how – we got to wash up first. What's the time by the clock?
R: Uh?
M: What's the time? (*Points to position of hands on clock.*) Yeah, what number's that?

R: Number two.

M: No, it's not. What is it? It's a one and a nought.

R: Nought – one and a nought.

M: Yeah, what's one and a nought. What is it?

R: There's one.

M: Yeah, what is it?

R: One – one and a nought.

M: What's one and a nought.

R: Um – that.

M: A ten.

R: Ten.

M: Ten to ten.

R: Ten to ten. (*Referring to face and hands of clock.*) Well, shall we wash then because they're not clean enough.

What we can see is a sustained conversation. We can also see how Rosie's mother is teaching Rosie about telling the time. Rosie is confident enough to respond to the time question imaginatively; she understands what it means, but she can't tell the time. You might think the final imaginative utterance is rather more creative than the 'correct response'. What we have is an example of natural conversation. You can see that Rosie and her mother take turns and that Rosie's utterances are not very much shorter than her mother's.

Let's look at the example of Rosie in school.

Rosie is making a Christmas calendar and there is an old Christmas card showing Father Christmas on skis (Ibid.: 97). Rosie (R) is being questioned by the teacher (T) and both of them are being interrupted by another child (AC):

T: (*Pointing at card.*) What are those things?

AC: Miss, I done it. Miss, I done it.

T: (*To Rosie*) What are those things?

AC: Miss, I done it.

T: (*Referring to skis in picture.*) Do you know what they're called? (*Rosie shakes her head.*)
　　What do you think he uses them for? (*Rosie looks at the card; the teacher turns to the other child's calendar.*)
　　It's very nice. After play, we'll put some ribbons at the top.

AC: What?

T: Ribbon at the top to hang them up by. Would you put all the cards together now? Put the cards together.

AC: Oh.

T: (*To Rosie, pointing at the skis on the card.*) What's – what are those? (*Rosie looks blank.*) What do you think he uses them for?

R: (*Rubbing one eye with the back of her hand.*) Go down.

T: Go down – yes, you're right; go on. (*Rosie rubs both her eyes with the backs of her hands.*) What's the rest of it? (*Puts down card.*) You have a little think and I'll get – er, get the little calendar for you. I think you're sitting on – Right (*points to calendar*), could you put some glue on the back there? (*Rosie takes the calendar from the teacher.*) He uses those to go down – (*five second pause*) – is it a hill or a mountain?

R: A hill.

T: A hill, yes, and what's on the hill?

R: Ice.

T: Yes, ice. They're called skis.

AC: Miss.

What happened to Rosie the conversationalist? Rosie offers just three utterances, the longest just two words. Can you identify in this short extract the way in which the regulatory discourse is entwined with the discourse of instruction? You might feel that Rosie's mother has the advantage of a one-to-one relationship, and of course she has.

Activity

Compare the two examples. Be careful, we can all behave like the teacher at very busy times.

Do you think it is possible for teachers to consistently use talk in the way that Rosie's mother does?

The short extract of Rosie with her mother is by no means unusual; it represents the high levels of linguistic skill that most children come to school with. The language is natural, and the interaction relaxed. We have commented above on the artificiality of school language; you can see that when Rosie is with her teacher. To reiterate, school language is different from out-of-school language – and sometimes this is because teachers have to interact with larger numbers of children all at the same time. But it is also caused by the way in which school knowledge is transmitted.

We said earlier that Basil Bernstein has pointed out how school knowledge is 'formal'. What he means is that we can set out what kinds of knowledge should be taught in a fairly precise manner. If you watch the film called *Kes* (Loach 1988), you will see how the boy hero cannot cope with the formal knowledge of school and yet he is able to learn the arcane mysteries of training a hawk. There is an interesting conundrum here; the boy is locked out of formal learning in school, both by the regulatory and the instructional discourse. From the school's perspective, he is inarticulate, but he is able to use his personal linguistic resources to make the formal stuff of falconry accessible. That knowledge is set down in a very precise way. The boy is not taught it; he acquires the knowledge by himself by practising with the hawk and reading a book. In school, he is taught knowledge in a classroom setting and the lessons proceed in a recognisable order; in the boy's school, knowledge is strongly defined and apparently context free. To return to Rosie, we can see that when she is with her mother the knowledge is domestic, familiar and contextualised. The teacher, because she is the teacher, has to control the knowledge and regulate the class; this leaves little room for Rosie to use her own linguistic resources.

We have drawn on the work of Basil Bernstein here because he offers a way of thinking about the consequences of language in use in school. His is a powerful and complex theory, but it has been and continues to be subject to critiques on both linguistic and sociological grounds. We will restrict ourselves here to linguistic critiques. Harold Rosen (Rosen and Rosen 1971) and Douglas Barnes (1977) make the point that schools seem to be disabled, in that they cannot make use of the linguistic resources that pupils have. Rosen argues that the code descriptions used by Bernstein, specifically his description of the restricted code, ignore the ways in which working-class speakers are proficient users of narrative. Both Barnes and Rosen argue that it is often the language of school that is restricted in the conventional sense and that pupils use language in a vibrant and meaningful manner but are rarely given credit for their creativity.

Edwards (1987) makes a rather similar point, arguing that:

> Bernstein's delineation of a gulf between the communicative experience of lower working class children and the chalk and talk of the classroom simultaneously underestimated the children and overestimated the classroom.

He goes on to say that it is most likely to be assumed by teachers and pupils that those being taught are essentially ignorant of the stuff they are being instructed in:

> This assumption brings severe functional constraints on the language pupils use, because what they can mean has be contained within the limits of what their teacher defines as being relevant, appropriate and correct.

We need to keep in mind this debate when we use Bernstein's work. What Edwards shows us is that the power of the teacher in defining not just *what* but *how* something can be said, cannot be ignored.

This is tied up with issues of regulation, control and the transmission of formal school knowledge. We will discuss them in detail as we turn to pedagogy, in future chapters. We began by celebrating and describing the talk accomplishments of children and related that to their experience of school as they become pupils. We have drawn attention to pupils' competence as language users and ended up by identifying the challenge of school language use for a substantial number of pupils. Our discussion and description of pedagogy is bound up with this challenge, and the dilemmas presented above and the way these issues are played out in classrooms.

Chapter 2

The importance of talk in whole class teaching

In this chapter, you will find:

- a summary of arguments about how primary teaching should be conducted
- a summary of significant studies that inform the whole class teaching debate
- something about classroom talk and educational success
- reference to research and relevant theoretical work you will need to be aware of to develop your own powers of research and reflection.

The difference between home talk and school talk is particularly apparent in whole class teaching, a setting for talk alien to the home. This chapter begins our discussion of whole class teaching and how it has and might be changed. It also raises the problem of why somewhere around 20 per cent of pupils gain little from their primary schooling. From the teacher's perspective, the majority of time in primary school is occupied by whole class teaching and has been since the introduction of mass education. While it is true that group and individual work are and have been used as a percentage of total time, they use very little of it. So it would not be unreasonable to ask why we need to spend time discussing what is an obvious thing and why we are urging teachers to do something they already do. In fact, what we need to do is to decide what *kind* of talk during whole class teaching will promote pupils' learning. We also need to be able to describe what *kind* of talk pupils use that will promote their learning. The language of whole class teaching is not simply a matter of the instructions that teachers give; it is also a matter of values, in that the relationship between pupils and teachers differs when we change the nature of talk. Put crudely, authoritarian teaching does not engender quality learning.

About whole class teaching

Improving the quality and quantity of pupils' classroom talk, and thus teacher–pupil talk, is often seen as key to improving classroom learning (Barnes, Britton and Torbe 1986; Rosen and Rosen 1973; Cazden 2000). Quality of this kind may be characterised by a focus on the use of language to explore new concepts and to initiate new ideas as well as a focus on learning outcomes.

A common sense view about improving the quantity and quality of language interactions between a teacher and their pupils is to focus on one-to-one relations. In some way, this focus arose from the idea that it was possible to model classroom talk on family talk. This common sense view, to some degree, dominated certain kinds of thinking about primary education from the late 1960s almost until the present. What was being stressed was the child as investigator and, at times, initiator and the teacher as facilitator and guide. In some cases this arose from a misreading and fundamental misunderstanding of the work of the psychologist Jean Piaget. This view was strongly criticised in the Alexander, Rose and Woodhead (1992) report as holding back the progress of many pupils. They put their criticism in very strident manner, saying 'primary school teachers are in the grip of an ideology'. It is our view that this kind of rhetoric is not appropriate in a supposedly 'cool' and analytic report, however they still present evidence that some teachers were pursuing the chimera of individualised education. We shall say more about this chimera towards the end of this book.

Unfortunately what was often inspiring and exciting learning and teaching has been parodied as the children doing exactly as they pleased and the teacher following. This view was often contrasted with the kind of whole class teaching that characterised primary education, particularly for 7–11 year olds in the 1950s. The idea here was that the teacher taught the class as an ability group, with the aim being to ensure that the maximum number of pupils progressed to grammar school. While children were taught in whole classes, where schools were large enough they were also streamed – that is, pupils were divided by ability using some kind of measure, most often competence in reading. In smaller schools, in-class ability grouping was the norm, a smaller-scaled mirror image of what was happening in larger schools. Research published in 1970 showed that the system of streaming was ineffective and this, coupled with the ending of Year 11-plus in most places, led to the abandonment of streaming – although ability grouping was still common. Regardless of whether the classes were streamed or of mixed age, whole class teaching was the norm and it has become part of teachers' and policy-makers' folk memory that things were better then because of the way teaching was organised.

The fierce polemical arguments about the virtues of teaching from the front as opposed to recognising the child as principal initiator have drawn on parodies either of the elementary tradition or of Plowden progressivism – which will be discussed in the next chapter – rather than examining the realities of what was going on in schools. Maurice Galton *et al.* (1999), in their measured book, summarise the debate and show how much of it is a matter of ideology not evidence. What Galton does is to review a range of studies, some of which we refer to in more detail below. His summary contrasts the nature of interaction in primary classrooms in 1976 with similar interactions in 1995–96. In doing this, he contrasts the experience of two real people: Donna, educated in the 1970s, and her daughter Hayley, in school in 1996.

> In 1976, typically, the teacher would have been moving around the room for most of the time talking first to one group of children then another, or to an individual child within the group. (Ibid.: 2)

> [...] in contrast to 1996 now they [pupils] seem to be always engaged in studying mathematics or English or preparing for the SAT examinations. Donna is pleased that Hayley is working hard, but she does sometimes wish that her daughter could have a little fun. (Ibid.: 29)

What has happened is a major shift towards whole class teaching/instruction. Donna remembers that it seemed more relaxed in her school days.

Our data show teachers working with the whole class most of the time, in particular they are teaching the whole class together. We can now look at how that situation has developed.

Neville Bennett's 1976 study *Teaching Styles and Pupil Progress* examined what was going on in a sample of primary school classrooms. As he showed, a good deal of whole class teaching took place, but pupils made most progress when teachers capitalised on one particular style. In short it was consistency in pedagogical approach that was the best indicator of good pupil progress.

The subsequent ORACLE study (Galton, Simon and Croll, 1980; Galton and Simon 1980) challenged the typology of teaching styles identified by Bennet and perhaps more importantly drew attention to the impact of teaching arrangements on teacher–pupil talk. The original ORACLE data were collected on fifty-eight teachers during 1976–78. What this data revealed was that when pupil–teacher interactions were viewed from the pupils' perspective, the majority of interactions occurred during whole class teaching. This seems paradoxical, that individuals get most attention in whole class settings, but it can be explained in this way. When the teacher is talking to and with the whole class, they are in fact addressing each individual pupil, but when they talk to one individual or to a small group, they are excluding the rest of the class from the interaction. However, it should be noted that the quality of classroom interaction is always enhanced by the presence of a skilled adult. In 1996 Galton and his colleagues revisited classrooms to look at pupil–teacher interactions in the same way. What they found was a decrease in one-to-one interactions and a slight increase in whole class teaching (Galton *et al.* 1999). They, too, found that the quality of interaction was enhanced through the involvement of a skilled adult. All these studies show that whole class teaching increases the quantity of interaction but they also show that the relationship between quantity and quality is somewhat tenuous. These data were collected before national policy focused on benefits of whole class teaching and, perhaps more significantly, before the introduction of the National Strategies for Numeracy and Literacy.

The early 1980s saw a major study of junior schools in inner London (Mortimore *et al.* 1988) which indicated that whole class teaching was rather more effective in relation to pupils' progress and achievement than individualised programmes of work or group work addressed to more than two subjects. Policy-makers could then turn to the evidence of the ORACLE and similar studies and evidence from what we now call 'school effectiveness' research to argue for a focus on whole class teaching.

Although in many places polemical in tone, and we shall return to this, Alexander, Rose and Woodhead's (1992) review firmly established whole class teaching as the way forward if schools were to meet central government's achievement targets. Policy-makers also turned to effectiveness studies which accounted for better achievement in Pacific Rim countries because of those countries' use of whole class teaching methods (OECD 1995). In the wake of all this, the pre-1997 Conservative administration set up a pilot project on whole class teaching for literacy, which rapidly became known as the 'Literacy Hour'. The 1997 Labour government established this as a National Policy, making it a very strong recommendation to schools and backing this recommendation with the threat of inspection. In the same year a Numeracy project was initiated. By 1999 all primary schools in England were expected to adopt the particular forms of whole class teaching set out in the *National Literacy Strategy* (NLS) and *National Numeracy Strategy* (NNS) documents for the teaching of numeracy and literacy. It was also argued that these kinds of whole class teaching methods should be used for teaching other subjects.

In part, the policy move towards whole class interactive teaching is also a response to the persistence of around 20 per cent of pupils falling short of success in their primary years. Of course, what constitutes 'success' is defined by government in terms of achievement targets. The introduction of whole class teaching in the interactive style has not changed this pattern of achievement. All the sociological evidence points to the fact that the majority of these 'failing' pupils are working-class and a significant majority of those are boys. Often the reasons given for this failure put the blame on the learner, as our discussion of Rosie in the previous chapter shows, but it is the language and organization of teaching that provides a major obstacle.

Why change?

This question of failing pupils has been a major concern of educationalists, politicians and policy-makers, certainly since the 1950s. What they and we can see is the way in which pupil performance is powerfully correlated with social class. This in turn may be compounded by race, ethnicity and gender. Simply noting this is not enough and we need to search for explanations. Although it may seem a diversion, it is important to sketch out briefly some of the things that have been suggested over time. One explanation offered for these correlations is that the intelligence of groups differs and that the less intelligent groups come from poorer socio-economic circumstances and that this is also true of some ethnic groups. At one point, regardless of the way intelligence was measured, it was claimed that males would naturally outperform females. These explanations were easily rejected (Rose, Lewontin and Kamin 1990; DES 1985).

Simply rejecting the above explanation did not change the relative performance of groups of pupils; other more powerful explanations were deemed to be necessary. Drawing on the methods and theories of anthropology, concepts such as 'cultural deprivation' and 'cultural disadvantage' were produced. An extreme example of this is the book by Oscar Lewis, *Five Families: Mexican Case Studies in the Culture of Poverty* (1975). In less extreme forms, these concepts were employed in England and Wales in the production of 'compensatory education programmes'. Such programmes sought to fill in the cultural gaps of pupils from disadvantaged backgrounds. In one of his earlier works, the sociologist Basil Bernstein criticised these ideas. The title of his essay is instructive, 'Education Cannot Compensate for Society' (1970). He remarks:

> The social experience the child already possesses is valid and significant, and this social experience should be reflected back to him as valid and significant. It can only be reflected back to him if it is part of the texture of the learning experience we create. (Ibid.: 346)

Often implicit in the cultural explanation was the idea of linguistic deprivation or disadvantage. It was proposed that the kinds of language that poor socio-economic group pupils brought to school was inadequate and did not enable them to comprehend the instructional form and content of classroom talk. Oddly enough, the idea of linguistic disadvantage often drew on the very early work of Bernstein, where he had proposed the idea of 'restricted' and 'elaborated' codes of language. As we shall discuss later, Bernstein developed his theories and argued that any view of his believing in linguistic deprivation was false.

What Bernstein seems really to be saying is that the organisation of school knowledge is what debars access to these kinds of pupils, as we discussed in Chapter 1. Gordon Wells (1981, 1987) conducted one of the largest studies of the home language use of children. He collected examples of the way parents and children talked and showed that, even for working-class children, talk was often rich and exciting, although this was often not recognised in school. We gave an account of some of Wells' work in the last chapter.

These explanations do not really offer a classroom solution to the 'problem', but it is argued that whole class teaching does. The evidence that whole class teaching increases the quantity of teacher–pupil interaction is well founded. You can see some of this evidence in later chapters.

What we need to consider is what kinds of talk actually go on in classrooms. In doing this, we will remind ourselves that not all classroom talk is about the subjects being taught. In addition, we need to think about the differences between classroom talk and ordinary social talk. Studies tend to treat classroom talk as natural. If we look at classroom talk, particularly the talk of teachers, we might better describe it as weird. When we looked at Rosie, we saw a remarkable difference in the way she interacted at home and at school. It seems classroom talk is weird for her, and that has consequences. Oddly, although for knowledge makes claims to be universal, the nature of classroom talk is context bound. Pupils need to know and understand the context of sch even of their own specific classroom, to make sense of what is going on.

Activity
Teacher talk and pupil involvement

Think about and observe what happens at the start of the school day.

Who talks to whom at the start of the day?

Who gets the teacher's attention as the social arrangements change during the first half-hour?

Whole class teaching prioritises talk and prioritises teacher talk. Why is this?

If we look at conversations, one of their features is the way in which speakers hop from theme to theme. For instance, we overheard two university students talking about an essay title as they were having coffee. They were joined by two friends who changed the topic to the television programme *Big Brother*. The theme rapidly became 'who was most fanciable' of the current male pop stars, and finally the group talked about the possibility of an end-of-year ball. Unlike conversations, classroom talk is usually themed and teachers who hop from theme to theme are often described as 'ineffective'.

Furthermore, we understand that in normal talk an invitation to do something – 'shall we' or 'let's just ...' – can be refused. The statement 'let's all sit on the carpet' or 'shall we go to the hall?' are more like commands which may not be refused. If we comment on someone's clothing, we are likely to say something such as 'that's a nice shirt', but in the classroom the comment probably goes like this: 'That's a nice shirt. How many different colours has it got on it?' These differences between natural conversation and classroom talk have been commented on by Mercer (2000). While conversation makes use of turn-taking, it is often overlapping and interruptions are allowable. Mercer sets out succinctly what he calls 'talking rules' for classroom talk. Note how different they are from the procedures of natural conversation.

> We share our ideas and listen to each other. We talk one at a time. We respect each other's opinions. We give reasons to explain our idea and if we disagree we ask, 'why?' We try to agree at the end. (Ibid.: 161–2)

Activity

In the previous chapter we showed how children's use of talk at home was very different from school talk. Here we are trying to get you to see how teacher talk in school is also different from that used outside school hours.

Classroom and school talk is weird.

Try statements like these in a meeting with your friends:

'That's a nice shirt. What kind of pattern would you call that?'

'I am thinking of something that takes cars across rivers, it begins with a "b" and is not a boat.'

What do you anticipate the response of your friends will be?

The social and organisational contexts in which talk occurs powerfully impact on the kinds of talk used. So different social contexts allow for looser or tighter thematic talk, as we said above and as you will have noticed in conducting the activities. One of the aspects of skilled teacher talk is the way in which it maintains a thematic unity while at the same time enabling pupils to express opinions and ideas. While this appears conversation-like, unlike social conversations it has the intention of increasing formal learning. This kind of skilled talk is often described as 'scaffolding' and draws heavily on Vygotsky's ideas of assisting pupil performance. We shall return to his ideas and the actions of teachers in later chapters.

As you will see, we argue and demonstrate that the talk of skilled teachers ranges across a variety of ways of talking with children. These discourses vary, but a common feature of the classroom talk of skilled teachers is the desire to assist pupils' performance and maintain order and discipline. Bernstein talks about the way in which different discourses intertwine and interact with each other. What he calls the 'regulatory discourse' is the one that teachers use to construct and maintain order in the classroom. But it does more than this; it establishes the relationship between the pupil, the teacher and the knowledge being transmitted. Pupils who rapidly grasp the strange statements that teachers use become identified as the ideal, the kind of pupils who will quickly learn. Sometimes the regulatory discourse comes on its own, but very often it is intertwined with the 'instructional discourse', and nowhere is this more apparent than in the teaching of handwriting.

T: Yes, it could be an 'i'. Now then let's do something a bit different. Watch because now it gets a little bit tricky. Not only do you have to get them to fit between those two lines, you also have to get them to curve at the bottom. Now before you do it, watch, it doesn't curve like that and it doesn't go like that, it goes like ... see if you can do it ... just carry on on the same line. (Eke and Lee 1991)

Here we can see how regulatory words and instructional words are put together in a seamless manner. The children are being taught how to behave as pupils – 'watch' 'carry on' – but at the same time are being instructed in handwriting skills – 'curve at the bottom'.

Taken out of the classroom, this bit of speech is distinctly odd. What the teacher is doing through this speech is both constructing the ideal pupil by regulating behaviour and teaching motor performance through both speech and practical demonstration. It will not have passed you by that the ideal pupil is both obedient and neat. What we have is talk that in social circumstances outside school would be regarded as entirely artificial. What we know from teachers' own accounts and from research is that some pupils enter school and are unfazed by the strangeness of school talk. They seem to know how it goes and what it means without needing lengthy explanations. Clearly these children have an advantage. They also comply with the content rules of classroom talk; they have some appreciation of what Bernstein is saying when he talks of 'classification' and 'framing'. We can see this because they know what an appropriate contribution to classroom talk is and understand who has the power to change the topic. They hand over the power of talk to the teacher. The other children are not linguistically disadvantaged; they simply operate in the 'real world' of talk, a world on the whole excluded by the artificiality of school and classroom talk, focused within curriculum boundaries. As we move on, you will see how teachers can overcome this 'difficulty' by making use of more conversational modes of talk and being prepared to engage with the pupils' definitions and decisions on the nature of the topic to be pursued – something usually called 'uptake'.

We can also see how these children are acquiring the habit of monitoring themselves at work.

T: I want to see who's clever enough to spot their own mistakes and if they've got one that isn't quite right put a little cross under it. Let's have look round. Let me see.
P: Mine isn't quite right.
T: Let me see if there's anyone has been grown up enough to find a mistake for themselves.
P: Yes, here's one.

The teacher appeals to the individual child's judgement of their own work by linking individual performance to 'universal' ideas of maturity and cleverness. Yet again we can see how the instructional and regulatory discourses come together. Bernstein has made the powerful point that not all schools and teachers enable all pupils to understand and respond to this kind of pedagogical talk.

What we have argued in this chapter is the way in which school and class-room talk is very different from everyday speech. It is, in fact, talk as pedagogy. 'Pedagogy' although a familiar term, sits a little uneasily in the lexicon of teaching and learning in the UK. Brian Simon defined it as 'the science of the art of teaching' (Simon 1981); what he means is that it is not a set of descriptive or prescriptive modes to follow, not a craft but an art. The working out of this art is best seen in the kind of talk skilled teachers use – talk that empowers pupils to express their own ideas; what Alexander refers to as 'dialogic teaching'. We also appeal to the powerful ideas of Basil Bernstein, who wants to add that an effective pedagogy is one in which the 'consciousness of the child is in the consciousness of the teacher' (Bernstein 1990) What Bernstein, Alexander and others are saying is that pedagogy is worked out in the classroom, it is an action or set of actions conducted by teachers and pupils. The creation of pedagogy is then in the realm of the teacher's professionalism; it cannot be defined by distant policy-makers. What we have experienced in England in recent years has been the attempt by policy-makers to interfere with the professionalism of teachers, to seize what Bernstein calls the 'pedagogic device'. Pedagogic communication is special; it is related to what is formally learnt in school. This communication comes about through the way teachers use talk to make the potential knowledge and skills actual in the classroom. Although this might sound grand, what we are saying is that through the pedagogic device changes in consciousness come about. Bernstein makes the point that the device is the ruler of this consciousness, so what teachers must do is become the rulers of the device. What this book is about is illustrating this device in action, so that you can know it and use it yourself. Policy-makers can and do define and describe the knowledge that should be taught; you can see it set out in the National Curriculum. The evidence to date demonstrates that their attempts to legislate for pedagogy have been less successful. We would agree with those we mention above that it is also improper to enact such legislation, in that pedagogy is created by the profession not its masters.

What else informs our view of pedagogy? The kind of classroom talk that we will show you is underpinned by the psychological ideas of Vygotsky and his interpreters. The key idea is 'social constructivism', which identifies the way in which language and action come together but also language in use as action in the classroom. This involves assisting pupils' performance through the selection, chunking and sequencing of classroom curriculum knowledge and the use of appropriate activity and talk. The national strategies provide good illustration of cultural selection chunking (the teaching objectives) and the sequence, year and term in which the chunks are to be taught. For the most vulnerable 20 per cent of the population, pedagogic attempts to direct how the material is to be taught have been unsuccessful. All of our subsequent discussions are variations of this theme.

Chapter 3

Children's experience
of primary school

In this chapter, you will be introduced to the following:

- the difference between individualised teaching and whole class teaching
- the way ideas about individualised learning are prevalent in the system
- large-scale studies of primary classrooms
- the way in which these studies might inform pedagogical change.

The problem that almost all teachers face, except those working in a one-to-one situation, is how to interact with and teach large numbers of children at the same time. In our everyday life, we do not have to speak with twenty-five to thirty people at the same time. If we did have to do so, we would think it very odd. School classrooms are then very unusual places. If we think school classrooms are ordinary, it is only because we have all experienced them. Let us give you an example of how different they would look if we had not had any prior experience. Craig Raine's poem 'A Martian Writes a Postcard Home' makes our world strange.

> Caxtons are mechanical birds with many wings
> and some are treasured for their markings –
>
> they cause the eyes to melt
> or the body to shriek without pain.
>
> I have never seen one fly, but
> sometimes they perch on the hand.

Did you guess that these are those familiar objects we call books?

We can make school equally strange. Imagine a Martian sent to Earth to discover how earthlings brought up their young. What would this creature notice and how would it report back to Mars? It would probably write something like this:

> Earthlings are very caring of their young. When they are born they are cared for by one person in groups of usually no more than two. There are some bigger groups and the largest I encountered was six young, but even here

most of the young were beyond the age of three Earth years. From birth to about the age of four Earth years, they are nurtured by one adult. At four Earth years, they are sent to live for a long part of the Earth day with at least twenty others and are cared for by one adult. Earthlings call this 'going to school' and the groups they are in are called 'classes'. It is very puzzling why they do this. I was told it was so the young could learn, but young creatures learn anyway. I will have to investigate further.

Alright, an unlikely scenario and not a very good joke, but still we hope it makes you think about what we do and why.

We all know that children go to school to learn school knowledge. For most of us, it is in school that we learn to be literate and numerate – learn history and science and geography and art, for instance. Outside school when we explain how to do something, we usually do it on a one-to-one basis thus allowing the learner to ask questions and seek clarification. In the case of practical skills, an apprentice has the opportunity to watch and model their actions on the work of the master and ask questions. It is not like that in school. Teachers are charged with teaching school subjects, the majority of which are not vocational, so they have to ensure that pupils understand why they are learning one thing rather than another. On top of this, they have to teach effectively a group of twenty-five-plus pupils!

One solution would be to treat the pupils as individuals. This seems like a common sense solution, since in families the youngest children learn a great deal and are treated individually. To go back to our example of Rosie, in Chapter 1: although she is from a big family, we can see her mum interacting with her on a one-to-one basis. You will have also seen how this encouraged Rosie to talk with logic and imagination. Even when the youngest children are in a big group before they enter nursery school, such as in a mothers' and toddlers' group, they always have mum with them and so interact individually. So what the teacher might do is mirror the activity of a caring parent and design work for each individual pupil. This is called 'individualisation' and has been recommended as the best practice for primary school teachers. Of the many documents that comment on primary education, the Plowden Report (CACE 1967) is one of the most important, because it set out an ideal way of teaching. It placed the child – not the curriculum – at the heart of education. If you look at the Plowden Report, you will see how much emphasis was placed on individualisation as good practice by the Committee.

At the end of the Report's Chapter 2, entitled 'The children: their growth and development', it sets out the implications of accepting what it argues is the nature of child development. Here are the first two implications:

> Individual differences between children of the same age are so great that any class, however homogeneous it seems, must always be treated as a body of children needing individual and different attention.

> Until a child is ready to take a particular step forward, it is a waste of time to try and teach him to take it. (CACE 1967, Chapter 2, para 75: 25)

As you can see, following these statements provides a tremendous challenge for the primary class teacher.

It is often assumed or claimed that there were a number of schools where teachers treated pupils as individuals and planned lessons on the basis of pupils' interests – ideal schools meeting Plowden's statements above. So teachers planned for individual work, often of an exploratory nature. More than that, in these classrooms the divisions between subjects were not apparent. Teachers did not plan English or mathematics lessons but took a theme such as 'water' and drew the subject knowledge out of that. Subjects were integrated and it was said that was the way children would learn best. For instance, Sybil Marshall (1966), usually held up as an example of this practice, illustrates examples of her work using history projects. Len Marsh (1970) evidences art and mathematics. The work described by these two exemplifies what is now called 'Plowden progressivism'. While it is true that many claims were made for this kind of teaching, there is scant evidence of it in practice. In fact, the Plowden Committee found hardly any primary schools which met the ideal set out above. Nevertheless it was perceived by some that the majority of primary school teachers did not teach subjects but left the children to explore their own interests and work in an individual manner. It was partly in reaction to this notion and to the school effectiveness research, particularly the work of Mortimore and his colleagues, to which we will return later, that whole class teaching has become the recommended manner of organising classrooms.

More recent studies, including Moyles *et al.* (2003) and Myhill *et al.* (2006) address the reality of primary school classrooms. They found, as did ORACLE and others, that the teachers spent the majority of their time teaching the whole class. But they go beyond this and seek to identify when and where teaching can be described as interactive. We will return to their studies and modes of analysis in the following chapter.

Schools dedicated to child-centred or learner-centred approaches have always had to work with the paradox that, while they wanted each individual pupil's needs to be prioritised, they still had to teach the 'basic subjects'. In 1975 Sharp and Green published a detailed study of teaching in a school dedicated to Plowden principles. These kinds of schools were and often still are termed as 'progressive'. They spell out the paradox in this way:

> As a progressive school, the children should be allowed to integrate their own knowledge, develop at their own pace, according to their present needs and interests. But the school also has to account for itself in the established way by teaching literacy and numeracy. (Sharp and Green 1975: 217)

A major constraint in pursuing this form of teaching is the fact that in most classrooms there is one teacher and at least twenty-five children. The ratio of twenty-five to one means that while the teacher interacts with the pupils for most of the class time, each pupil's interaction with the teacher is for a minority of their class time – an interesting paradox.

What evidence is there for how teachers teach, what their teaching style is? Style is clearly related to pedagogy. If we look to a period when individualisation was promoted heavily, the post-Plowden era, we can select a seminal study. Bennett (1976) sought to discover how teachers taught and how their style related to pupil achievement. Bennett collected his data in 1973. At this time it was assumed that large numbers of teachers would have adopted individualisation and child-centred approaches. His analysis revealed that this was not the case, and that pupils who were taught in a more structured fashion – by subject rather than by topics, and as classes rather than as individuals – made greater progress.

The ORACLE project, conducted between 1976 and 1980, which we introduced in Chapter 2, provides detailed evidence of the nature of classroom interactions. The study recorded what teachers were doing and what pupils were doing. So the study showed what subjects pupils were learning and how much time they actually spent on tasks. The researchers recorded every 25 seconds who was talking and to whom. They used two records: one for pupils and one for the teacher. Here are some data from the teacher's record. The resulting analysis shows in stark relief the unequal distribution of talk, as you can see.

	Pupil	Teacher
Percentage interactions	15.8	78.4

In a one hour session, this figure (15.8) amounts to a total of nine minutes, twenty nine seconds.

What these figures demonstrate is the well-nigh impossibility of individual instruction in primary classrooms. The follow-up study conducted by Galton *et al.* (1999) shows the same stark contrast between pupil and teacher interactions. What it also shows is an increase in group and whole class interactions as against individual interactions. In brief, we are saying that although individualisation is a good and useful teaching strategy, in practice it is not possible.

Paul Croll puts this very succinctly:

It is clear from the figures [percentages of teacher–pupil interactions] that however much teachers try to increase their individual interactions from their already high level, there can only be a very small impact on any individual child's experience of one to one interaction with the teacher. (Croll in Croll and Hastings 1996: 20)

Activity

Get someone to observe you teaching and try the following, which is based on the Teachers' Record from the ORACLE study.

Every 25 seconds code what is happening under the following descriptions. You may find it helpful to make a table like this, in which each cell equals 25 seconds.

Interactions	1	2	3	4 etc
Teacher interacting yes/no				
Interacting with whom				
About what				
Teacher activity when not interacting				

Probably the most influential study of primary teaching is the one that focused on what we now call 'school effectiveness', conducted by Mortimore and colleagues in junior schools in the Inner London Education Authority (ILEA). Research evidence from Mortimore *et al.*'s (1988) seminal study points to a clear relationship between whole class teaching, single subject teaching and higher pupil achievement. The study casts into doubt the efficacy of individualisation. Subsequent work in school improvement and school effectiveness studies has similar findings. Anecdotal comparisons (Reynolds and Farrell 1996) with Pacific Rim practice argue that whole class teaching is key to raising achievement in primary schools.

Concerns to develop whole class teaching (e.g. Alexander, Rose and Woodhead 1992) chimed with Brian Simon's 1985 complaint that primary education in England focused on individualisation at the expense of developing pedagogy. Simon famously asked the question 'Why no pedagogy in England?' and answered it by saying there was too much attention given to individualisation. Simon (1985) defines pedagogy as the science of the art of teaching. What pedagogy is about is not the needs and interests of individuals, but methods which seek to ensure that all pupils can learn formal school knowledge and it is to the development of this that we now turn. The examples of research that we have given are important for your understanding of the principles on which whole class pedagogy may be built. These studies provide the foundations on which whole class teaching methods were and are being constructed.

Whole class teaching almost inevitably means that the teacher and the class will focus on one curriculum subject. This enables teachers to organise knowledge in a way that makes it clear to pupils what they are learning. It also enables both the teacher and the pupils to identify what has been learnt. So each subject is clearly defined as a separate set of skills, facts and activities. Both pupils and teachers can say, 'before play we were learning maths but now we are doing English'. Knowledge in this case is strongly classified, and the fact that pupils and teachers have an understanding of what is being and what has been learnt tends to make the pedagogic process rather more visible. Strong classification of this kind is associated with clear sequences of instruction, strong framing. Classification and framing are key concepts about how knowledge is organised and delivered in schools; they derive from the work of Basil Bernstein, to whom we referred earlier when we talked about codes. So classification is about what will be talked about and learnt, and framing is about the order and way in which it will be talked about. We will return to these ideas in later chapters, particularly when we address the teaching of literacy and mathematics.

The advocacy for whole class teaching, which became apparent in the mid-1980s and has been pursued ever since, is related to the research work summarised earlier. It can also be seen as the only possible organisational response to the demands of the National Curriculum. The National Curriculum was written in such a way that pupils were expected to learn specific subject content over specified periods of time, and this was enforced by assessing all pupils at the ages of seven and eleven and by the inspection system after 1992. Although the curriculum has undergone two relatively major revisions, these have reinforced the separate subject nature of the curriculum and the specification of what is to be learned over what period of time. The decision to create a curriculum composed of traditional and recognisable subjects has caused major difficulties for those holding a belief that subjects are not important for primary school children. This belief argues that children learn in a wide variety of ways but do not differentiate knowledge by classifying it, as we said earlier. It is eloquently expressed in the Plowden Report:

> The school ... lays special stress on individual discovery, first hand experience, and opportunities for creative work. It insists that knowledge does not fall into neatly separate compartments ... (CACE 1967, para 505)

But to reiterate, even when teachers were apparently following a child-centred ideology, they were caught in what Sharp and Green (1975) identified as the central paradox. In a study of a school dedicated to the Plowden ideal, these researchers showed how teachers found it almost impossible to derive mathematics and reading and writing – subjects they had to teach – from within the child. The teacher then had to intervene to name the subject. In Sharp and Green's terms, teachers are caught in a paradox: they believe in following one method, but the nature and structure of what they have to do forces them to follow the opposite method of teaching.

Today the logic of a prescribed national curriculum which defines the subjects to be taught and their content militates against subject integration and the kind of loosely structured organisation of knowledge often described as 'topic work'. This move towards strong classification and framing marks a shift in the way that primary teachers in England think about teaching. The belief (ideology) that all learning emanates from the child's natural curiosity and interests is not really tenable in a system that defines knowledge and prescribes the order in which it is to be taught.

Whole class teaching is not a panacea. Individualisation is not possible, even if desirable, and whole class teaching brings its own challenges and problems. There is a clear danger that in whole class teaching pedagogy is developed on the principle that 'one size fits all' – and this brings as many problems as it solves, in that some pupils learn more quickly and some more slowly than others. To be effective, whole class teaching must have the flexibility to plan for group activities as well as whole class activities.

Activity
Discussion with teachers

Talk to a teacher or teachers in the school and ask them something like the following:

Do you think it is best to teach children individually?

Are there any children whom you believe can only be taught as individuals?

When do you use whole class teaching?

Why do you use whole class teaching?

Pedagogical initiatives

In July 2004 the Secretary of State presented to Parliament a document entitled *Department for Education and Skills: Five Year Strategy for Children and Learners*, the primary strand of which built on a previous document, *Excellence and Enjoyment* (2003). In the former document, teachers are advised to take 'a more personalised approach to the curriculum', but to do this by using the 'successful *Primary [National] Strategy* [the combined successor to the *Literacy* and *Numeracy* strategies]'. At first reading, it would appear that teachers are being advised to move away from whole class teaching and towards some kind of individualisation. We have shown that such an approach is well-nigh impossible. So what are teachers actually being told to do? The *Primary National Strategy* document makes the following bold statement:

> Every teacher knows that truly effective learning and teaching focuses on individual children, their strengths, their needs, and approaches which engage and motivate them. (DfES 2003: 39)

Here there is a real tension between the tight framing and classification of literacy and numeracy and the drive for indivualisation. Content for both is set out by age group, by year and by term. Although teachers are advised to use assessment to identify targets and tasks for individual students, the concerns of politicians and policy-makers remain the overall achievement levels of each age group. The then Secretary of State, like his five predecessors from the same party, was concerned to ensure that 80 per cent of students at the end of Key Stage Two (KS2) meet their achievement goals. It was in order to meet these goals that first the *National Literacy Strategy* and then the *National Numeracy Strategy* were introduced.

Since the introduction of the two strategies, advice and guidance to teachers from the Department for Education and Skills (DfES), now Department for Children, Schools and Families (DfCSF), and other official and quasi-official bodies has been to employ whole class teaching. It has been argued that not merely is this more efficient in terms of teachers' time and effort, but it better focuses the teachers' attention on overall achievement goals. In brief, whole class teaching is much more likely to ensure that 85 per cent of pupils achieve the specified levels in literacy and numeracy by the time they are eleven years old.

So teachers are being asked to meet national targets by adherence to what is now a national strategy setting out in detail content and teaching method, whilst dealing with pupils at the level of individual need. To underline this, in both literacy and numeracy teachers are strongly urged to teach the same content in the same way to all pupils and yet to use assessment as a 'powerful tool for making sure that learning fits individual needs'.

Activity

In your observations and conversations with a teacher, try to discover if individual needs can be addressed through whole class teaching.

Have a conversation about the importance of SATs scores and what the teacher believes about them.

This activity will lead you into the next chapter and will raise these important issues:

How do experienced teachers find ways to respond to individual needs during whole class teaching?

What sort of linguistic repertoire is needed to ensure the inclusion and engagement of all pupils?

In this chapter, we have shown you how a variety of studies describe what happens in primary classrooms. These studies revealed that Plowdenite progressivism was very rare. What Bennett, Sharp and Green and ORACLE showed was that, in fact, the majority of teaching was not highly individualised. Teachers taught whole classes and dealt with groups. They also show the asymmetrical relationship between teacher and pupil talk. Sharp and Green (1975) identify a further problem with individualisation, in that:

> whilst the teachers display a moral concern that every child matters, in practice there is a subtle process of sponsorship developing where opportunity is being offered to some and closed off to others. (Ibid.: 218)

Mortimore's study, using some of the observational methods of ORACLE, went further and argued that it was more effective in terms of pupil learning to teach following a tight curriculum focus and using whole class teaching. The introduction of the National Curriculum pushed teachers into dealing more explicitly with single subjects, and the demands of assessment meant that all pupils had to have the opportunity to learn those subjects. The introduction of the strategies explicitly demanded whole class teaching accompanied by very focused group work. The strategies also prescribe in some detail the content of the subjects, English and mathematics, that must be covered and the time frame over which they should be covered. The strategies focus on the nature of teaching and, to a large extent, prescribe how teaching should be conducted – they are a pedagogical package addressed to teachers and teaching. Even so, we believe that experienced teachers find ways to respond to individual needs during whole class teaching by developing a sophisticated linguistic repertoire aimed to ensure the inclusion and engagement of all pupils. This is an important aspect of interactive whole class teaching and is discussed in the following chapters.

Chapter 4

What does an effective whole class pedagogy look like?

In this chapter, you will be introduced to the following:

- how to describe and analyse classroom talk
- how the analysis and description of classroom talk helps us to create a pedagogy
- the idea of 'scaffolding'.

We argue that an effective and successful pedagogy reaches most of the pupils most of the time, and it includes all of the pupils. Such pedagogy meets a number of the criteria for inclusion. We will argue that what is most significant in all of this is classroom talk, that is the talk of the teacher and of the pupils.

In order to describe and justify this pedagogy, it is necessary to be able to describe and analyse classroom talk. In the previous chapter we drew your attention to classroom interaction studies, which show the pattern of verbal interaction. These studies show, for instance, the amount of time that teachers talk for and the amount of time that pupils talk. All of them show a pattern like this: at least 70 per cent of classroom talk is done by teachers, leaving 30 per cent for the pupils. Studies also show how often teachers use questions and how often pupils respond. In brief, these kinds of studies enable us to compare the talk of teachers and pupils by counting their occurrence. What these studies do not try to do is to describe the qualities of teacher and pupil talk. What we will now go on to show is how it is possible to describe and analyse key qualities of classroom talk. It is necessary to be able to do this if we want to establish what a good pedagogy looks like. We argue further that you need to be able to do this in order to improve your own practice.

The description and analysis of classroom talk has a relatively long history. Smith and Hardman (2003) review a substantial number of studies conducted over recent years. From ORACLE we learnt about the patterns of classroom talk – about who spoke most, and how and to whom they spoke, and what they talked about and the sorts of questions that teachers ask. What ORACLE and similar studies do not try to do is to identify the meanings that teachers and pupils are making in classrooms. Different sorts of studies try to indicate how pupils and teacher make sense of the places in which they spend their working lives. Probably the most famous of these focusing on English primary schools is Andrew Pollard's *The Social World of the Primary School* (1985). Pollard shows how talk has special meanings for pupils and teachers which may be rather different from everyday use. Studies like these enable us to understand the way in which people in schools interact in a social manner.

What we are interested in is the way that talk relates to learning – how teachers and pupils use talk in the classroom to learn, and how pupils in particular use language to learn things. Connie Rosen (1971) provides an inspiring example of how pupil talk leads to excitement in learning.

> Gaynor asked whether Miss Collins had been talking about schools in the Middle Ages, we thought about Jane's Granddad, who had come in to see us the previous day and how old he was and decided with the help of blackboard and chalk that he was four years old when the school had begun and could have been in the babies' class. They collected dates and details like squirrels. Rosen (Ibid.: 22)

This is an example of good primary practice communicated with enthusiasm and clarity but it's difficult to use as a model. This is because what Rosen does not try to do is categorise rigorously the sort of utterances she recorded. This makes it hard to learn lessons from her studies. It is difficult to carry her analysis into personal professional practice.

Activity

Sinclair and Coultard identify the IRF structure as a general description of the way that lessons go. This includes the kind of lectures and other classes you attend.

Here is an example to follow.

Initiation	What do you think 'scaffolding' means?
Response	Well, erm, it's when the teacher sort of supports the child.
Follow-up	Do you mean supports them when they are learning something new?

Now record about ten minutes of a seminar and identify initiation, response and follow-up.

What did you find out?

Repeat this when you teach a class yourself.

Sinclair and Coulthard (1975) present a model of the way in which lessons are structured and offer a basic structure which is common to all classroom talk. They describe teaching as following this sequence: initiation, response and follow-up (IRF). That is, the teacher starts the idea or theme and usually through questions gets pupils to respond, and then the teacher gives the pupils feedback (follow-up). This basic structure is followed in most lessons and, as you can see, talk is dominated by the teacher who occupies at least two-thirds of the time available. Although IRF sequences are common to most lessons, we can learn more about them by looking in detail so we can ask, for instance, what kind of initiation is used.

A good way of looking at IRF sequences in more detail and of thinking about how talk sustains learning can be found in the metaphor of 'scaffolding'. Both David Wood (1998 2nd ed.) and Jerome Bruner (1986), drawing on Vygotsky's ideas, use the metaphor as an explanation and description of the processes of supporting learners when they are learning. When you build a house, you have to put down foundations; these foundations are crucial if the building is to stand up. As you begin to build, you use scaffolding and this scaffolding enables you, the builder, to reach the developing height of the building. But the scaffold also functions to support the brickwork while the cement and other bonding materials harden and dry. What we have just said celebrates the use of scaffolding in a particular way. Scaffolding, though, has other uses: sometimes we use it to repair a building, to stop buildings from collapsing, and also as the backbone of barriers designed to keep people out. It is worth bearing all this in mind when you read or hear the word 'scaffolding' used to describe what a teacher is doing.

The term 'scaffolding' is often used to describe certain kinds of talk, especially when teachers can be heard to be actively trying to push children's thinking along. The metaphor is derived from the work of Vygotsky and his students and followers. Vygotsky emphasises the fact that although learning is an individual thing, it can only really go on in a social context. For Vygotsky, learners use talk to learn and they learn in and through talk. He uses the now-famous phrase 'Instruction leads development' (Vygotsky 1986), which prioritises the role of the teacher and teachers' talk/speech. The commonest manner in which teachers instruct is through talk. Much of this talk can be described as scaffolding pupils into new knowledge. Talk is central to the enterprise of teaching and learning.

It would be wrong to suggest that learning comes about best if pupils sit silently and listen to teachers. In order to take ownership of new knowledge, pupils need the opportunity to put things into their own words. In the case of scaffolding, we can say that pupils by talking to each other and responding to the teacher are scaffolders of others' learning. Even so, scaffolding is too global a metaphor to enable us to understand what is going on in effective classrooms. In order to do this, we need a more finely grained description.

A number of workers have developed systems to describe, categorise and ultimately analyse classroom talk. Mostly these systems focus on teacher talk. We have drawn on a range of approaches, attempting to balance the attention paid

Table 4.1 Approaches to scaffolding: Tharp and Gallimore (1988) and Mercer (1992)

Assisting Pupil Performance Tharp and Gallimore (1988)	Scaffolding Media Learning Mercer (1992)
Modelling Psycho-motor – physical demonstration Cognitive demonstration – ways of thinking about the classroom task	Introducing concepts, terms and styles of discourse which might serve as models for pupils' own work
Contingency management –managing pupils' behaviour (e.g. keeping pupils on task)	Not mentioned
Feeding-back	Evaluating and legitimising children's responses and contributions in terms of their relevance to the curriculum
Instructing – telling pupils what to do	Not mentioned
Questioning	
Assessment questions	
Checking pupils' learning	
Assisting questions – intended to provoke new thinking	
Cognitive Structuring Type 1 – structures of explanation	
Helping pupils to organise ideas in ways new to them	
Cognitive Structuring Type 2 – structures of cognitive activity	Using shared experience (of TV) to explore children's understanding (of what they saw).
Helping pupils to understand how to organise ideas	Paraphrasing and reformulating to check understanding and make meanings clearer.
Not mentioned	Eliciting children's responses so that individual responses are shared.
	Helping children to focus on educationally significant aspects of events.
	Helping learners to perceive continuity in their learning by relating things said and done in earlier events.
	Not mentioned
	Relating classroom activities to other cultural reference points outside the classroom – that is, to what everybody in the classroom knows because they talk about it outside school (for example, the TV series *Big Brother*)

to teacher talk and to pupil talk. Tharp and Gallimore's (1988) work, we think, is critical for enabling us to show what is happening when teachers teach. Rather than using the global description 'scaffolding', they have differentiated the ways in which teachers assist pupil performance. They recognise that talk is complex and that very often teacher talk functions in such a way that it does more than one thing.

In Table 4.1 you can see the kinds of descriptions and categories used by researchers in America (Tharp and Gallimore 1988) and the UK (Mercer 1992).

For the purposes of the classroom talk, we will be analysing a combination of these approaches based on Tharp and Gallimore's (1988) account supplemented by Mercer (1992). The value of prioritising Tharp and Gallimore (1988) lies in the categorisation of kinds of teacher talk. As we noted above, Tharp and Gallimore do not present their categories as discrete but rather 'The means of assistance are necessarily intertwined, occurring in combinations and sometimes simultaneously' (Ibid.: 47). Here are some specific examples of these categories in use. These are the categories with which we began our analysis and description.

Modelling – showing pupils how to do things

Psycho-motor – physical demonstration by the teacher.

T: We start at the top, we come down and we flick up.
T: Alright, notice something I-'m going to take the decimal points out here.

Cognitive demonstration – ways of thinking about the classroom task

P: Erm, because we just put the noughts in and added it all together but we put the points in the wrong place.

Contingency management – managing pupils' behaviour (e.g. keeping pupils on task)

T: Right, if you have an orange booklet in front of you then write your full name and school on the front top, please.
T: Right, OK now, where are your eyes supposed to be?
P: I'm going first.
T: Shshsh, hands up.
T: Right, everyone altogether.

Feeding-back

T: Very nice drawing being done here, very careful.
T: Good boy, zero point zero one, now I'm going to write them in columns.

Instructing – telling pupils what to do

T: You haven't measured it well. Let's measure it quickly. Put it on there.

T: See if yours matches up with what we've got on the board.

Questioning

Assessment questions – checking pupils' learning

T: What do you notice between bread and cereal?

Assisting questions – intended to provoke new thinking

T: Do you think Goldilocks was right to eat the porridge?

Cognitive Structuring

Type 1 – structures of explanation, helping pupils to organise ideas in ways new to them

T: You had to change the axles because the other axles wouldn't let the wheels go round OK, yes?

Type 2 – structures of cognitive activity, helping pupils to understand how to organise ideas

T: There are odd numbers and some special odd numbers, so three and seven aren't like nine.

A key problem for understanding classroom talk is the nature of question used. In Tharp and Gallimore's (1988) case, it transpires that many apparent 'assisting questions' turn out to be requests for correct answers. Young (1992) helpfully identifies a series of teacher and pupil turn-taking, that help bring clarity to the question/answer process. Here are Young's categories:

What Do Pupils Know? (WDPK)

WDPK1 – Teacher reminds and checks.

T: Do you know what else is made from milk?

WDPK2 – Pupils reproducing what has been taught

T: What's the first thing you do when you paint a landscape?

Guess What Teacher's Thinking? (GWTT)*

GWTT1 – Demonstrates teacher control and illustrated by an emphasis on answers worded correctly. It is common in new work and development stages.

T: So perhaps we could think of // quickly put it as a question. We could say what …?

GWTT2 – Terminology guessing. The teacher expects children to guess what is in their head. The practice is embedded in other utterances and may involve clue-giving.

T: We could call them 'protein' or we could say …
T: A surprise, Mark, what's the proper name for a surprise, Mark?

Discursive (D)

D1 – Teachers work with children to make things clearer. They also use talk to collaborate with children in solving problems and seek pupil involvement in paraphrasing and the confirmation/disconfirmation of statements.

T: Thank you, who's going to put that in their own words? Hayley, yeah?

D2 – Teacher inquires into what the pupils think or feel.

T: Right OK, how the world got here, right over to you, what are your thoughts?

Uptake

Closely associated with discursive utterances is the notion of uptake (Nystrand *et al.* 1997). We take this to be the acceptance and following-up of one pupil's ideas by the teacher or other pupils who incorporate them into subsequent talk.

T: Ah now, Amy said something interesting there, 'your soul'. Right now, just let's think about that for a second. All of you, just look this way a minute, where is your soul?

* // indicates a break of two seconds or more, / is less than two seconds.

Evidence of cognition

All teachers want to know that when pupils are talking they are thinking, they are learning through talk. Oddly enough, evidence of this often comes through repetition, pauses, 'ums and ers' and 'you knows'. During the course of this sort of talk, pupils occasionally create overarching ideas.

Speaker nomination

Our own work has shown us that nomination is very significant. By this we mean when a teacher or a pupil invites a response by naming an individual. At times this is an aspect of power, as it is when the teacher uses both the regulatory and instructional discourse. In some classes, but only some, pupils are encouraged to nominate but this rather rare.

Activity

Here are some examples of classroom talk, between teacher (T) and pupils (P).

Using the categories above, describe what is happening.

A Year 2 class

T: What other foods can you find to help your body grow? That have got proteins.

P: I know.

T: Yes, tell me.

P: Fish, nuts.

P: Peanut butter.

T: Well, not strictly peanut butter. Beans, different kinds of dried beans.

P: Eggs.

T: Eggs.

P: Milk.

T: Milk.

A Year 6 Class

P: Yeah, we give / we tell one part of Hamcroft but we don't the other / we just show the tidiness of Hamcroft / that our town's history and everything and that it's tidy but we don't show where most / where on the other parts of the town it's really messy and untidy / we just show the tidiness of the town / we only showed one street / that was all / just the high street / and there's more places where it's untidy / and not history erm / they built new houses / being built and everything.

P: Yeah.

P: Now the fields are going.

P: New estate.

P: Just new homes now.

P: Yeah.

P: We made it look like it was a nice sweet town and it was very quiet.

P: Yeah.

P: But it's not / there's lots of cars and lorries go through.

There are some more mundane ways to describe classroom talk which nevertheless may be significant. Most obviously, who is speaking: the teacher, another adult, a pupil girl or boy, pupils, pupils categorised as having special needs or being bi-lingual, for instance? We can also count the length of utterances to see who gets the longest and shortest turns.

As well as knowing how teachers and pupils talk, it is important to know what they talk about. Teachers have to transmit school knowledge – the content of the various subjects that are specified in the National Curriculum. In addition, there is the subject knowledge required of the *Primary National Strategy* (literacy and numeracy) and that specified by Standing Advisory Committee on Religious Education (here-after SACRE) following the Qualifications and Curriculum Authority (QCA) for religious education. We have coded talk by matching what teachers and pupils say to the learning outcomes of the strategies and those set out in Qualifications and Curriculum Authority (QCA) documents. For science and for ICT, we have used the QCA schemes of work and teachers' plans. This is a convenient way of coding the content of lessons.

We are able to code what teachers and pupils talk about, how they talk and how much they say. This does not cover everything that happens in classrooms, nor everything skilled teachers do. Moyles (Moyles *et al.* 2003) and her co-workers remind us of the complexities of the classroom and how teachers plan to meet those complexities. Although it is not possible to code for many of these things, they are significant because they are the context in which teaching and learning proceeds. According to Moyles *et al.* teachers take cognisance of the following:

- assessing and extending pupil knowledge
- reciprocity and meaning
- attention to thinking and learning skills
- attention to pupils' social and emotional needs/skills.

Any description of good practice must take account of these aspects of teachers' thinking.

What we have shown you is a way to describe classroom talk. It may look complicated but, in fact, it isn't. The detailed discussion of lessons in Part Two of this book uses the framework set out above. Other researchers such as Moyles *et al.* (2003) and Myhill *et al.* (2006) use frameworks that focus on interaction, scaffolding and learning; they have similar concerns to ourselves. If you look at their frameworks, you will find helpful alternative approaches to thinking about how teachers talk.

As you can see, we are arguing that talk is vital in the production of an effective pedagogy. Of course, productive talk implies productive listening, so another way of thinking through the importance of talk is to consider speaking and listening. The importance of speaking and listening for children has been recognised for many years. Policy-makers and advisors to teachers have produced extensive documents demonstrating the importance of speaking and listening. These documents urge teachers to provide 'space' for pupils to speak, listen and respond to both the teacher and each other.

The National Curriculum from 1989 onwards has prioritised speaking and listening. But let's take the example of one year, 2003. In that year, the government strategy paper *Excellence and Enjoyment* (DfES 2003) was published, building on the success of the well-embedded literacy and numeracy strategies and seeking to improve the support 'they provide on speaking and listening'. In its wake, the QCA published four documents devoted to speaking, listening and learning, all of them arguing that good teaching requires the extensive use of speaking and listening. *Speaking Listening and Learning Key Stages 1 and 2 Handbook* (QCA 2003) states very clearly that 'excellent teaching of speaking and listening enhances children's learning and raises standards further'. The document talks about interactive situations where meaning is mainly constructed collaboratively; they designate this as 'discussion'. Even so, by 2005 Ofsted were still commenting unfavourably on the use of speaking and listening in English lessons:

> Too little attention has been given to teaching the full National Curriculum programmes of study for speaking and listening and the range of contexts provided for speaking and listening remains too limited … in too many classes, discussion is dominated by the teacher and the pupils have limited opportunities for productive speaking and listening. (Ofsted 2005: 1)

As we re-emphasise below, the use of orality is still a major challenge for us as teachers.

Alexander (2004) uses the term 'dialogic' and sees this as being more than simply discussing issues; for him, 'dialogic teaching harnesses the power of talk to engage children, stimulate and extend their thinking, advance their learning and understanding'. In this case, speaking and listening are powerfully connected to the learning of formal school knowledge, not simply to ways in which children can respond to teachers' questions. Key to this is reciprocity, which requires teachers to listen to children's ideas and consider alternative view points. Myhill *et al.* (2006) show that there is little evidence for this kind of pedagogy and this chimes with our own findings; where we do find it is in classrooms with very highly skilled and perhaps unusual teachers. What we are saying here is that this kind of teaching is a challenge for the teacher, but equally it is a challenge for the pupils, who are not accustomed to this kind of pedagogy.

Excellence and Enjoyment (DfES 2003) is a response to the criticism that the literacy and numeracy strategies were stifling teacher creativity, that they were creating a pedagogic orthodoxy which at all times prioritised the teacher as the transmitter of knowledge. You can see by reading the 2003 handbook on speaking, listening and learning, that the role of the pupil is considerably advanced. The handbook makes very strong arguments for a pedagogy that moves away from simple transmission and towards forms of dialogue.

> We are convinced that excellent teaching of speaking and listening enhances children's learning and raises standards further. Giving a higher status to talk in the classroom offers motivating and purposeful ways of learning to many children, and enables them and their teachers to make more appropriate choices between the uses of spoken and written language. (QCA 2003: 4)

In the discussion papers associated with speaking and listening and entitled 'New Perspectives on Spoken English in the Classroom', speaking and listening are seen to be more like the kinds of conversational discussions that we have and less like the answering of teachers' questions.

Mercer (2003) makes the point in this way:

> For children to become more able in using language as a tool for both solitary and collective thinking, they need involvement in thoughtful and reasoned dialogue, in which conversational partners 'model' useful language strategies and in which they can use language to reason, reflect, enquire and explain thinking to others. [...]
> Providing only brief factual answers to IRF exchanges will not give children suitable opportunities for practice. (QCA 2003: 76)[1]

Alexander's (2004) emphasis on reciprocity, which is akin to the above, moves us further away from straightforward transmission; his argument for dialogic teaching necessarily prioritises some form of equality in dialogue, changing the role of the teacher quite radically. Despite this, formal school subject knowledge is still prioritised. In the chapters that follow, we will show you how teachers talk in classrooms, and how that talk relates to subject knowledge. We will also show you, by using our frameworks, some examples of how skilled teachers use talk to promote learning. You will see when you read those chapters how the form and content of teachers' talk guides the ways in which pupils talk and what they talk about.

---

1 The documents referred to were published by QCA and are well worth detailed reading. Unfortunately they are not available in their entirety on the QCA website so you will need to get them from your library.

Part Two

In this part, the chapters are about how classroom talk operates when teachers are teaching different subjects. We show you examples of what happens in real classrooms. In Part One we described the sorts of ways that researchers have analysed and described classroom talk, and you will see here that we use those studies as well as our own work. In each chapter you will see in detail how we have analysed what happens and then used that to try to identify the principles that underpin particular pedagogical practices. You will see that we have used the methods and framework we set out in Part One to describe classroom discourse in detail. In doing this, we show how teachers talk differently when teaching different subjects; although these differences may be subtle, we argue they are important. There are also subtle differences in the way different groups in the classroom are talked to and this enables us to identify aspects of differentiation in whole class teaching. We show, too, how we can describe points at which children are actively learning. By doing this, we are able to suggest how teachers might improve their language use in whole class lessons. Of course we are not saying that this is the only way to engage pupils in effective talk for learning, but we can say, with confidence, that engaging in talk in this way is likely to be very productive.

It will not surprise you to notice that we have focused on the core curriculum of mathematics, science and English. Alongside this we have put a particular emphasis on the *Primary National Strategy* at Key Stages 1 and 2. Much of our data were gathered before the point at which schools were implementing the *Primary National Strategy* and were still following the *National Numeracy Strategy* and *National Literacy Strategy* and their accompanying supplementary documentation. You will probably find that a large number of schools retain this emphasis. We have also focused on ICT and religious education. We focus on the former for a number of reasons, perhaps the first being the way in which national policy has put ICT and the need for all pupils to gain knowledge and skills of it at the centre of the educational agenda. It is also clear that the use of ICT permeates not just school learning but learning outside school as well. More contentiously, we can say that being able to use ICT changes and expands the way pupils think. The case of religious education is interesting and important, because in many schools it is the subject through which pupils learn about personal moral issues as well as trying to understand what spirituality means for them and others. As a consequence, quality of talk in these lessons is rather different, as you will see from our research.

As we said in Part One, this book will help you to meet the standards set for newly qualified teachers. The following general description indicates the content of standards which you will cover, in such a way that changes can also be met. It will help you to adopt innovation in a creative manner and to create classrooms in which you can personalise learning and provide opportunities for all pupils to learn effectively. You will be able to use the examples and the method of analysis to develop your curriculum planning and to identify different pedagogical strategies to meet the needs of all pupils. The chapters make clear the differences between statutory and non-statutory frameworks and how you can use and adapt them.

In each chapter we have offered you vignettes of teaching and a fine-grained description. This description draws on carefully considered research methods and frameworks you saw in Part One, especially in Chapter 4. As you read each chapter, we believe you will deepen your knowledge and understanding of how classroom talk may be researched and, more importantly, how you can harness the results of that research to improve your own classroom teaching. We are convinced that the vignettes give you an opportunity to analyse the quality of language used and thus discover the quality of highly skilled teaching in the subject areas presented. We have deliberately focused on highly skilled teachers working in challenging circumstances, often with large numbers of pupils with additional needs. This enables us to explore with you the work of teachers who make a real difference to pupils learning through classroom talk and, of course, other aspects of pedagogy.

The chapters deal with specific subjects but also let us discuss the use of particular kinds of classroom talk and its consequences. Each chapter shows you how skilled teachers use formative assessment to inform their teaching and to adapt that teaching to maintain a dialogue. Chapter 5 is about the teaching of literacy. You will find accounts of the way in which two teachers deal with the requirements of the then *National Literacy Strategy*. As well as gaining insights into how these skilled teachers work, you will be able, both through reading and conducting the activities, to develop your knowledge and skills as a reflective practitioner. Chapter 6, about religious education, shows how teachers are able to facilitate pupil talk that focuses on universal questions of great significance. In this chapter, you will see how this classroom talk is based on recalling and discussing, and how pupils can seize the agenda and skilled teachers cope with the jumble of talk that follows. Chapter 7 shows how learning and engagement can be checked and a dialogue opened in a subject, mathematics, where the teacher is traditionally the fount of all knowledge. Chapter 8 highlights the opportunities for engaging with discursive talk while using ICT. The final curriculum chapter in Part Two again shows skilled teachers and includes them using forms of assessment to engage the pupils in a dialogue about science. We conclude with a discussion of match, differentiation and personalised learning and an overview of the case we have made in this book.

You will find that we suggest there are lessons to be learnt and we try to spell those out succinctly.

Chapter 5

Checking and discussing
– teaching literacy

In this chapter, you will learn:

- how good and effective teachers focus their utterances on cognitive outcomes
- how to seek to include all pupils
- to skilfully use questions to challenge pupils to think
- to make effective use of nomination.

We now turn to the classroom practice of the teaching of literacy. In 1997 a major change in the way that teachers should teach literacy was introduced. Detailed documentation spelling out both content and teaching methods was sent by the Department for Education and Skills (DfES) to each classroom teacher. The documentation was detailed, extensive and explicit, and additional documentation was added to the original package on an almost yearly basis. The most striking aspect of the original documentation was the way in which the hour devoted to literacy was set against the clock. Originally segments of the hour were given over to particular aspects of reading instruction following these components:

- word-level work – phonics, spelling and vocabulary
- sentence-level work – grammar and punctuation
- text-level work – comprehension and composition.

In a sense, this notion of strictly following the clock and the documentation was at odds with the way English primary school teachers had previously viewed their role, but the experience of the National Curriculum, its attendant assessment and Ofsted inspections, had made the teachers much more biddable.

The original Literacy Hour clock (Figure 5.1) begins with half an hour of whole class teaching and concludes with another ten minutes of whole class teaching as a plenary session. The effect of using Ofsted inspections meant that whole class teaching was 'enforced' on all schools. This needs a little consideration. Up until this point, the Secretary of State and the Department had always maintained that it was not their role to tell teachers how to teach. When the then Secretary of State Kenneth Baker (in Haviland 1988) introduced the Education Reform

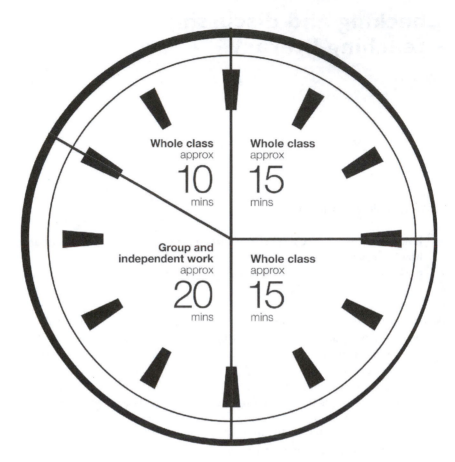

Figure 5.1 The Literacy Hour clock

Act (hereafter ERA) into the House of Commons, at its second reading he said explicitly that it was not his intention to tell teachers how to teach nor would it be right for him to do so. Subsequently the Department published guidance and commentary on the new curriculum and re-emphasised this position:

> The legislation does not allow particular textbooks or teaching methods to be prescribed as part of a programme of study. (DES 1989: 4.15).

Regardless of all that, we are now in a position where whole class teaching is deemed to be both essential and effective. The research we drew on earlier indicates that whole class teaching is effective. Yet, when it was pushed through by the Literacy Hour document, it was not presented as the result of evidence but rather as the result of a powerful political drive based, at best, on anecdotal descriptions. Earl *et al.* (2003), in their evaluation of the twin strategies, make this very clear. They point to a general acceptance of the strategies and talk about policy levers of change but offer no systematic review of research evidence supporting the pedagogy set out in the documents. The easy acceptance and sometimes 'ritual' following of the documentation because of its tight prescriptivism was to be deemed a problem in that it stifled creativity, a point to which we shall return.

A depressing feature of the education system over its existence has been the fact that 20 per cent of pupils gain little or nothing from their schooling. This persistent 'long tail' of underachievement by socially disadvantaged pupils was a major reason for the introduction of the Literacy and Numeracy hours. The challenge that teachers faced, and continue to face, was how to engage the 20 per cent in productive learning. This was recognised by the then Prime Minister Tony Blair and regularly returned to by his first Secretary of State for Education, David Blunkett. Blair said, reflecting on the 'long tail':

> we have been good at educating an elite at the top but ... the imperative to raise standards for the many in line has been neglected (in Earl *et al.* 2003: summary, 4)

Blunkett, on 13 May 1997, said:

> That's why today I am announcing that by the time of the national tests in 2002:
>
> - 75% of 11-year-olds will be reaching expected standards for their age in maths, and;
> - 80% will be reaching the standards expected for their age in English.
>
> ... The place to start the recovery is in primary schools. (Press release statement by Secretary of State, Department for Education and Employment, 13 May 1997)

The principal way in which the targets in literacy were to be met was by teachers implementing the literacy strategy.

We have already argued that the way to make a difference for the many pupils rather than the few is to make use of particular forms of classroom talk. In the rest of this chapter, we will discuss our own research. It was conducted in classrooms where skilled teachers were teaching pupils in challenging economic and social circumstances. These teachers demonstrated how they could work with pupils to produce effective learning and engagement with school tasks. The lessons we comment upon show teachers using the literacy strategy but each of them does it in a less programmatic manner than the original document envisaged. We now turn to looking in detail at what these teachers do and what lessons we can learn from them.

The classrooms, the teachers and the children

Purple Class

This is a Year 2 class with thirty-four pupils on roll, of whom fifteen were identified by the school and other agencies as pupils with special educational needs. Although the percentage of pupils with special educational needs (44%) was well above the national norm (26%), the proportion of girls and boys with special educational needs reflected the national picture (Croll and Moses 2000). The school served a well-established municipal housing estate and also drew pupils from other rented and owner-occupied housing. A relatively high proportion of pupils came from families in straitened economic circumstances. There was also a relatively high percentage of pupils from single-parent households, almost all female householders. This can be seen from the number of pupils entitled to free school meals, 65 per cent, a recognised reliable proxy for family poverty. Family poverty and pupils identified with special educational needs make the teaching a major challenge; these circumstances would also predict that pupils make much slower progress in all subjects, but particularly in literacy.

It's Wednesday 10.45 am, and the children come into the class after playtime and hang up their coats. The class teacher, Sheila, calls them to order and tells them to sit on the carpet; they do this. There is a big book displayed on a stand in front of the carpeted area. The teacher sits on a chair in front of them, theatrically rolls up her sleeves for work and asks, 'Where should your eyes be?' 'On the text', the children chorus.

What's happening here? The rolling-up of the sleeves is the teacher's personal way of establishing it is time to work. But it is more than this, as it is culturally significant, too. The working-class culture these pupils have grown up with recognises this signal as showing that work has begun. It is not at all unusual for someone to say 'let's roll up our sleeves up and get on with it [a task of some kind]'. This is an extremely effective and efficient management strategy using non-verbal signals. But how can we interpret the children's response to what seems to be a typical infant classroom management utterance (contingency management)? Their response shows that they know they are to attend not just to the teacher but to the text as well. Sheila here combines both the regulatory and instructional discourses; in the case of the regulatory, she models it by the action of rolling up her sleeves. Knowing the word 'text' is important since it establishes an aspect of formal school knowledge and reflects the way in which the documentation directs teachers to use technical vocabulary. The documentation presents very strong 'classification', a term you have come across in previous chapters. In following the document, Sheila uses strong classification and strong framing. 'Framing' here refers to the way that Sheila makes the lesson proceed in a systematic manner, as you will see later.

The lesson proper began, with word-level work, when Sheila told the children what they were going to do. During literacy teaching on the previous Monday and

Tuesday, the class had already engaged with the study of the 'ea/ee' phonemes – part of a long sequence of lessons about vowel phonemes. Work on the 'ea' phoneme began briskly, with Sheila saying 'I've got a list here. Which ones go in there?' Now let's look in detail at what Sheila was doing. She used contingency management (regulatory discourse), ensuring the conditions were right for teaching and learning. The move between control and teaching is seamless, the instructional discourse is intertwined with the regulatory where necessary, but the highest percentage of Sheila's utterances are instructional. Let's look at a sequence of the actual discussion between the teacher and the children.

P: Protein.
T: Lucy?
L: Meat.
T: Meat, Lucy, how do you spell 'meat'?
L: M-E-A-T (*Naming the letters.*)
T: Good girl. Speak slowly, so I can hear.
L: M-E-
T: And it's got the little word in it.
C: 'Eat'.

What we can learn from Sheila is to cover the instructional aspect quickly, using the minimum number of utterances when covering this kind of content, instructing and checking what pupils know. So, she signals the start of the lesson by rolling up her sleeves, a powerful non-verbal signal. She then asks the children to look at the text; this utterance is about management and content. In this lesson, over 70 per cent of Sheila's utterances are focused on learning outcomes; these are word-level outcomes, 'ea' phonemes, other phonemes and high-frequency words. What this involved was a return to previous work, a revision of word-level work on phonemes and teaching the recognition of high-frequency words. It is this clearly focused use of language that enables Sheila to be effective and efficient. In this use, she demonstrates that she does not expect a great deal of discursive talk from the pupils because that is not the aim of this lesson. We can see a rapidity of utterance use; each one is relatively short but always to the point. The children recognise that they are being reminded of what they know. When she nominates pupils, she is attempting to ensure they are engaged with the content. We note that she nominates boys more often than girls for these sorts of questions, thus keeping them on track. She is differentiating the task along gender lines, so it is no surprise that boys visit a wider range of learning outcomes. The transcript in the activity box illustrates Sheila at work.

Activity

Look at this fragment of teaching and find examples of word-level work. Identify the form of utterance being used.

T: E-A-T! Eat! And these are some more words we've been looking at. Do you remember we said there is something that has got lots of protein in it and it's also/it's good for you because it helps you grow//It's got the word 'eat' in it. You eat//

P: Protein.

T: Lucy?

L: Meat.

T: Meat, Lucy, how do you spell 'meat'?

L: M-E-A-T (*Naming the letters.*)

T: Good girl. Speak slowly so I can hear.

L: M-E-

T: And it's got the little word in it.

C: 'Eat'.

T: You eat meat. Now, Danny, you told us yesterday didn't you how we spell the **other** meet.

C: When you look

T: No, I'll ask Danny. Why don't you put your hands up?

D: M

T: Good boy.

D: E

T: Meet people.

D: E

T: Good boy.

D: T

T: Well done.

D: Meet.

T: Sometimes we've got the long 'e' being made with/which two letters? And sometimes we've got those being made by the long 'e'.

C: (*Unison.*) Eee!

Sample word-level questions in your own teaching and the teaching that you observe.

Does this content lead to particular forms of questioning and talk?

Sheila wants to get the pupils to think about the difference between questions and statements. She does this by getting them to turn statements into questions; this time she uses the form of 'Guess what I am thinking?' The effect of this is to encourage the children to use the correct canonical form. Here again, she is matching the way she talks with the pupils to the content she is addressing. Unlike during word-level work, Sheila does not nominate particular pupils; one result of this is that pupils respond in unison and Sheila is happy for them to do so. In this brief time span, we can see Sheila employing flexible but properly targeted teaching strategies.

In the case of focusing on reading, the class is using an information text about nutrition. Sheila's utterances show the same brisk pace that she used in the earlier section of the lesson. We think this is more challenging for the pupils, because she is asking them to exercise some kind of judgement. They, in turn, produce longer utterances and slightly more discursive ones. She also reduces the pace slightly and this is associated with the use of more interwoven contingency management utterances, usually focused on boys. What Sheila is doing is drawing on formative assessment to try to ensure that all the children are engaged with the task. Changing the pace slightly enables those with special educational needs, and boys, to stay with the lesson content. Again you can see Sheila doing this in the transcript set out in the activity box.

Activities

T: Do you think it would be easier to read the book without headings? Can you tell what this page is about through looking at the headings? Let's read this heading. Ready.

P & T: (*Unison.*) Food that helps you grow.

T: Does that help you read, when you look at the picture and then look at the heading?

P: Grow.

T: Who thinks 'yes'?

P: (*Unison.*) Yeah, yeah.

T: Who thinks it's a good idea?

P: (*Unison.*) Yeah, yeah.

P: Food helps.

T: To have it in your writing, perhaps. Let's look at this heading. Ready?

Look at this and identify how it seeks to include all the children. Look carefully at the teacher's utterances to see precisely how she ensures inclusion.

In Purple Class there are a high percentage of pupils identified as having special educational needs, and as is the case nationally, there are more boys in this category than girls. Pupils with special educational needs are regularly called on, nominated; this strategy keeps them involved. But Sheila does more than this. She restricts the number of learning outcomes she expects them to respond to, but ensures they meet those outcomes that are core.

Drawing on her knowledge of the pupils, the learning requirements of the strategy and her personal experience of teaching literacy, she prioritises phonemic discrimination in this lesson.

Her next priority is discriminating syllables for the pupils with special educational needs. There is evidence that phonemic and syllable discrimination are very significant for the development of reading, particularly for pupils who experience difficulty with the task (Adams 1990; Chall 1970; Goswami and Bryant 1990). This evidence has led to a prioritisation of systematic phonics teaching in the *Primary National Strategy*.

P: Beam.
T: A beam you walk along in PE [physical education]
P: I know.
P: (*Unison.*) Beam.
T: Michael, what do you remember?
M: B-E-E- (*Naming letters.*)
T: Ellis?
P: (*Unison.*) E-E ... E-A.
E: E-A.
T: E-A, you saw and remembered well, and//a weed in the garden?

Sheila is carefully differentiating the content to be covered. But she does more than this. In her interactions with pupils she is constantly reminding and checking the pupils' understanding by asking them to reiterate what they have been taught. So the pupils are regularly revisiting what they have learnt.

Activity
Select an aspect of word-level work, phonological awareness, word recognition, vocabulary or handwriting. In doing this, have an age group in mind. Then, construct a teaching script to guide your verbal interactions when teaching this aspect, what you say in the first ten minutes. Code the script using the codes given at the beginning of the book. (pp. 36–8)

What does this tell you about your planned teaching of this area?

Blue Class

This is a Year 5–6 class with thirty pupils on roll, of whom fourteen are identified by the school and other agencies as pupils with special educational needs. Again, the percentage of pupils with special educational needs (47%) was well above the national norm (26%), although the proportion of girls and boys with special educational needs reflected the national picture (Croll and Moses 2000).

The school serves a well-established working-class suburb on the edge of the city. The teacher is male.

It is Wednesday, after assembly but before playtime. The children are sitting so that they can all face an overhead projection screen beside which the teacher sits. Projected onto the screen is a newspaper article.

As soon as the children are settled, copies of the article projected on the screen are distributed. This is done with quite remarkable rapidity by paper copies being passed from hand to hand with minimal disturbance. The end of the distribution of the article is the signal that work has commenced.

What we can see is minimal contingency management. The teacher, Graham, and the pupils engage almost immediately with the tasks in hand. When we coded the teacher's utterances, only 6 per cent were coded as contingency management, regulatory discourse. Overall 90 per cent of the talk in this lesson could be coded for a literacy learning outcome, a point to which we shall return. The teacher introduces the camera operator and indicates they will be able to talk to him after the lesson. In doing this, he ensures the pupils' attention to the task rather than to the camera operator. He told the children what they were going to do, and in doing so also reminded them of the work completed on Monday and Tuesday.

T: Stop there. Excellent! What are we looking at? What sort of piece of writing are we looking at already? Ebony?

E: At a newspaper.

The children had individual copies of the newspaper article which was also displayed on the overhead projection screen. They were examining the nature of persuasive writing (text level) and were investigating spelling rules (word level). The content of text-level work was particularly demanding because of its sophistication. What they were being asked to do was bring an understanding of the nature of newspaper articles, genre and text type, in order to go beyond merely reciting what was in the text. They were being asked to say how the writer persuades and what kind of thing the reader was being persuaded into. One result of this was some mismatch between Graham's utterances and the responses of the pupils. In the case of spelling rules, the match between the form and content of teacher and pupil utterances in contrast, was very close. Even so, there was clear evidence that the pupils engaged with the analysis of this text.

T: Thank you. Who's going to put that in their own words? Hayley, yeah?

H: It's saying while prisoners are in jail, but they're getting computers/um/um and two million pounds spent on them, but they're not in jail.

T: Good girl, sorry go on.

H: And they have to work in worse conditions.

Activity

Identify an age group and find a persuasive text suitable for you and the children.

Identify what you would want the children to learn from studying this particular text. You will now be in a position to identify learning outcomes from the strategy that will be met. This lesson will be about word-level work, vocabulary and text-level work, comprehension and composition. Make a sequenced list of questions you would ask about the text. You should identify word-level and text-level questions.

Will you plan a lesson that teaches word-level work separately from text-level work? Can you identify word-level and text-level change-over?

What are the reasons for the decisions you have made?

In Blue Class on this morning, as we said before, 90 per cent of the utterances used by both teacher and pupils were on task. What this means is that these utterances were related to learning outcomes and not to classroom management and control. What we have is an example of a lesson in which the instructional discourse is prioritised. This is a remarkable phenomenon. It is characterised by the skilful use by the teacher of utterances that are targeted to assist the pupils in their learning. It is worth noting the differences in the mean utterance lengths between pupils and teacher. The mean utterance length used by Graham was 27.2 words while over half of the pupils had a mean utterance length of less than six words, but of course the mean utterance length for pupils was greater than this. Conventionally this difference in utterance length between teacher and pupils would lead to a conclusion that there was little discursive talk in this lesson. In fact, 16 per cent of the teacher's utterances were coded as discursive against 24 per cent of the pupils' utterances. There is an important lesson here: it is not simply the length of utterances or the balance between length of pupil and teacher utterance but the quality of those utterances that counts. In other words, wordiness is no guarantee of discursive talk, although longer pupil utterances are often associated with it.

Currently there is a major concern, nationally and internationally, about the way in which boys lag behind girls in their literacy accomplishments. Much research work claims to show that a contributory factor to this is the way boys disengage with literacy tasks – crudely, do not join in the lesson. In this lesson we do not find this, 48.6 per cent of pupil utterances were produced by boys and 38.9 per cent by girls. Whatever other research shows, here the boys are engaged with the lesson and they volunteered more regularly than the girls. This is interesting in that there are a lot of boys with additional educational needs in this class and the teacher's discourse encouraged these pupils to engage with literacy learning. They were encouraged to involve themselves in 'reading' the text, to investigate spelling rules and to apply their common cultural knowledge to the text. Turning to the girls, although collectively they are invited to speak as often as the boys, they do not volunteer to speak as often as them. When they speak, they say more, with the mean utterance length for girls being eleven words while for the boys it was just below seven. Again, it is not the quantity but the quality of the utterances that is important; perhaps the girls make more considered responses than the boys.

In contrast to Sheila, Graham makes little use of utterances of the type 'guess what I'm thinking?', but like Sheila he is keen to check what the pupils are learning and, in doing this, is keeping them focused on the task. He uses the checking form particularly when he is discussing word-level work, as did Sheila.

At the level of text work, Graham is faced with a more challenging teaching task, and as a consequence he cannot employ utterance types which ask pupils to identify canonical forms. He is engaging the pupils in the exploration of the nature of the genre of this particular text. He makes use of discursive utterances to challenge the pupils to identify the linguistic and the rational nature of persuasive texts. In order to ensure that the pupils are able to engage with the task, Graham is unafraid to slow the pace of the lesson. So he uses longer utterances and often visits only one learning outcome. An important consequence of this is that he gets longer pupil utterances.

Lessons to be learnt

Good and effective teachers focus their utterances on cognitive outcomes. They make sure their talk is on task and expect the pupils to follow this example. In the case of Graham, we can see that clearly in the percentage of utterances related to learning outcomes. But it is not just that he refers to the content; it is also to do with the nature of the utterances. His consistent use of assessment questions in relationship to word-level work and discursive utterances related to the structure and nature of the persuasive genre they were dealing with. Whole class interactive teaching makes good use of checking, i.e. formative assessment questions and interim summative questions.

In order to maximise the inclusion of pupils with special educational needs, Graham links learning outcomes to everyday knowledge; for instance, he asks these pupils to use their knowledge of school buildings to help them to relate to the article. He is also prepared to ask shorter questions and to make more use of formative and interim assessment utterances. Like Sheila, he makes careful use of nomination. A result of all this is that pupils with special educational needs are prepared to risk volunteering answers to questions addressed to the class as a whole. One consequence of this is that boys volunteer to speak more – an interesting contrast to the claim that boys disengage with literacy tasks.

In both classes there were a high proportion of pupils with special educational needs. A major challenge for the teacher is not simply to include them but also to ensure they are meeting the learning outcomes to some level. To help them achieve this, teachers use nomination. This has a tendency to move the lesson towards a form of individualisation, and this produces a differentiated pace. By this we mean that all pupils experience a change or difference in pace.

Chapter 6

Recalling and discussing in religious education

In this chapter, you will learn about how skilled teachers:

- avoid closed questions
- prioritise opportunities for discursive talk
- use weaker framing than in core subjects
- use different talk when they are teaching about main faith traditions than when they are dealing with puzzling questions.

As a subject, religious education has a very curious position in primary schools. It is declared to be part of the primary school basic curriculum in the original 1988 Education Reform Act (ERA), notwithstanding that teachers, pupils and parents are protected by the *Education Act 1944* from any compulsion to engage with the subject. Yet national policy has been insistent on its presence in schools. It is not, nor has it ever been, a national curriculum subject, but like a national curriculum subject it has national syllabus and guidance documents. It is the responsibility of local committees known as SACREs to agree upon and write the syllabus, and this syllabus applies in non-denominational schools. Such syllabuses must not be designed to convert pupils or to urge a particular religion or religious belief on pupils (*Education Act 1944*, Section 26 (2)). There is an expectation that you will know something of the content of the subject and how to teach it, and that is reflected in the Standards, but teachers are still protected by the 1944 Act from any compulsion to teach it.

The QCA (1994) have produced model syllabuses and in doing this have specified learning outcomes. In 2004 they revised the framework to develop the 1994 document but maintained the previous learning outcomes. These learning outcomes are more general and open than those specified in the *National Primary Strategy*, largely because of the strictures of the law as noted above. The two QCA syllabuses are indicative of two distinct approaches to religious education in non-denominational schools in England.

> Model 1 is structured around the knowledge and understanding of what it means to be a member of a faith community.

Model 2 is structured around the knowledge and understanding of the teachings of religions and how these relate to shared human experience. (QCA 2004)

Above we pointed out that you are expected to know the content of the syllabus and how to teach it. But what you are expected to do is to teach about the religion(s), not to teach religion. This is a very important point because it means that religious education lessons are not like any others in the primary curriculum, and we will now outline why. In the preceding chapter, you have read how teachers teach phonics, phonemes, genre and text types. They do not simply teach about them but teach the pupils the nature and functions of the above and check that the pupils have learnt them. It is not just a matter of being able to describe the phoneme 'a', but of teaching it successfully so that, if tested, the pupil can demonstrate knowledge. It is not a matter of opinion but of the facts of linguistic science. In the case of mathematics, two plus two are always four in the decimal system, and the answer cannot be a matter for discussion, because it is the correct answer. What we have in these two subjects is strong classification, since the boundaries and territories of the subjects are very well defined. When teachers teach them, as we have shown in previous chapters, they are also strongly framed. We discussed this concept and the concept of classification in Chapter 3.

Religious education provides an interesting and challenging subject in the way it is set out in the QCA syllabus. In the case of the content, the 'what is to be learnt'; it is not a matter of correctness, the content is open to discussion and interpretation.

Activity
Make a quick note of the content you have seen in at least two religious education lessons. How difficult do you think the ideas are? Do you think that primary aged children are able to deal with such complex and abstract notions?

Also try to find out what the pupils talk about during religious education lessons.

The non-statutory guidance (QCA 2004) talks about 'learning about religion and learning from religion', but not learning a religion. What we have is very weak classification; the content is not codified in such a way that teachers are expected to teach testable items, as they are in mathematics and English. Pupils may be expected to know that in Islam the five duties are often described as the five pillars, but they are not expected to accept either these tenets or their claims to truth; they simply need to know *about* them. As a consequence of this, the teacher cannot lay claim to the right answer and it is a matter for debate and discussion. The very fact that the syllabus insists on discussion as a major pedagogy means that the lessons are weakly framed; the teacher can be led by the pupils' opinions and judgements. You can see how different this is from almost every other thing taught in schools. You might also note how questions about the environment and matters of life and death become part of the religious education lesson.

In our discussions of classroom work, we shall refer to work on 'Living faiths today' as main faith traditions and work on 'Questions and teachings' as puzzling questions. 'Living faiths today' describes the different religions most likely to be encountered in the UK. 'Questions and teachings' explores how religions relate to shared human experience. The classes provide a number of challenges to the teacher and to the nature of teaching. As in the other cases we have used, these teachers have been identified as experienced and skilled practitioners with high professional standards.

The classrooms, the teachers and the children

In two classrooms we examined the teaching of 'puzzling questions'. Both classes were taught by men, one a Year 2 class and one a Year 5–6 class. These questions are deemed to be the sort of things that people have asked over time, such as: What happens after you die? or Are humans uniquely different from all other animals? These questions might be answered by reference to religion or not, but in essence they are matters for discussion not matters of fact. In two other classes we examined the teaching of a main faith tradition, the teaching about religions. In a Year 3 class taught by a man, the focus was on Judaism and in a Year 5 class taught by a woman, the focus was on Buddhism. Although committed to the teaching of the subject, none of the teachers claimed to be specialists in religious education.

Puzzling questions

Gold Class

It's Tuesday morning after playtime. The Year 2 children come back into the classroom and the teacher settles them very quickly and asks the children to recall what they have been learning in science and in religious education around the theme of 'life'. He writes their responses on the whiteboard. The discussion is lively and ranges over some interesting topics, such as who the hero of *Raiders of the Lost Ark* is and whether dinosaurs died of boredom. The teacher (T) allows wide-ranging ideas at the beginning, thus showing the pupils (P) that they can introduce their own ideas.

P: Some people, when they die, they get thrown into snake pits.
T: Err, well, it might be your imagination or on what's the name of that adventurer who goes in to look at tombs.

P: I know.

P: Errr, Tomb Raider.

T: Not Tomb, the bloke who goes.

Later:

T: Could it have happened to the dinosaurs?

P: Yes.

T: Yes.

P: The dinosaurs died.

P: Dinosaurs can't feel things.

A feature of this lesson was the way in which the teacher enabled the children to talk and set the direction for further discussion. Only 27 per cent of pupil talk related to relevant learning outcomes. Children's talk ranged over both science and religious education, as did the teacher's talk; what we have is weaker framing than in some other curriculum areas. The teacher does not try to exclude children's ideas. The content is open to interpretation and change, unlike in a lesson on number facts. As the lesson developed, the theme of signs and symbols began to become apparent. The talk was not idle chatter but explored difficult questions. The children are trying to make sense of the idea of special days and signs and symbols.

P: If //

T: Yes?

P: If // we don't if / the lollipop lady didn't have any to put signs up the cars would crash and the special days were and the special days were if if somebody's wants to go to a wedding you can't send em it off because it won't be a special if you can't call it a special day.

Here we can see the teacher enabling the children to engage with the themes and thus creating the opportunity to explore ideas through language.

Activity
Look back over your evaluations of religious education teaching. Find any examples of the kind of pupil talk like that above.

How would you go about enabling children to use talk in an exploratory manner? In thinking about this, it would be helpful to identify the kind of talk that silences children.

In the same lesson as above, the teacher made great use of common knowledge. One result of this is rather lengthier pupil utterances than we observed in other curriculum subjects. There were forty-five pupil utterances of eleven words or more. Most studies show pupil utterances to be much shorter than this, and utterances of this length occur much less frequently than here. The teacher is happy not simply to give feedback but to take the pupils' ideas and use them to engage in a dialogue. Here is an example:

P: Em, er, I know what Sally was talking about the cross with the circle one, the one where we was going on a trip and I saw it.
T: You saw it? Marvellous/ Gracey F?
GF: So people think that God is real?
T: ... So people think/ I ought to write these up. Shall I write them up?
P: Yeah.
T: OK, so we all die/ die / lollipop / I'll just write them in, em er, shorthand. What was yours, er em, I have forgotten, er, what was yours Liz?
L: To live.
T: Live. What did you say? To make God real?
P: No, I said to make people think that God is real.

The teacher comments that this is an important distinction.

First you will note how remarkable this exchange is. It moves with great rapidity between different but related topics, and the teacher acknowledges the importance of all the topics and encourages pupil intervention. Then a seven-year-old corrects the teacher and presents a provocative statement about the relative nature of belief in a Godhead. If we use the jargon of curriculum assessment, this pupil is performing way beyond the expectations set out in the QCA guidelines. This kind of classroom discourse uses discursive questioning but becomes an intellectual dialogue. Here a pupil is prepared to tentatively offer an understanding of life and death.

P: Erm ... When you die, sometimes you believe that you will be put in a fire.

The pupil distances herself from the belief and uses hypothetical language. As with the example above, this kind of reasoning is not expected of pupils of this age. Some authorities would argue that seven-year-old pupils are neither capable of such understanding nor able to express such things with logic and clarity. In fact, there is now received wisdom that children at this age are not 'ready' for such arguments as this, based on research conducted in the late 1960s (Goldman 1965).

The QCA materials do not focus on the question of death, but these pupils – like many others – want to discuss it and their teacher enables them to do so. We need to be able to describe what the teacher does so that this kind of dialogue can happen. First, the teacher recognises that the way talk goes cannot be defined in advance. This is about asking genuinely discursive questions; it's also about the tolerance of the jumble of talk that struggles for meaning and a willingness to respond to answers that others make. Doing this, of course, makes maintaining the themes of the lesson very challenging. What is needed is careful, patient listening and management.

Silver Class

It is Thursday afternoon. A Year 5–6 class is sitting in the library. The teacher begins the lesson by asking the pupils to draw on their common cultural knowledge – things they have learnt from television, magazines and social talk as well as previous learning in science and history. They go on to discuss the evidence record for human ancestry.

P: The teeth.
T: Teeth, good, what would the teeth tell us? That would be in the skull,
      wouldn't it, but what would it tell us, Emma?
E: If the people used to eat meat or vegetables.

They then go on to discuss those people's concerns and the ways in which religion might have helped them respond to puzzling questions. As with Gold Class, the framing of the subject 'religion' is relatively weak, and the content is very much the pupils' agenda.

   About a third of the total lesson talk related directly to the QCA learning outcomes. Of this total talk, 36% of pupil talk could be described in that way. The classroom discourse ranged very widely, covering science, the origins of the planet, and ancient history – particularly life in ancient Egypt.

P: Do they think that God done it?
T: Indeed, they believed in God, yes. Which direction do you think they'd look
      to think about God, which direction, Josie?
J: Up in the sky.
T: Up in the sky. What would have made them really wonder when they looked
      up in the sky? What sort of things would they have wondered about, /
      Adam?
A: Stars.
T: Good, stars, excellent, at night certainly. What else might, during the day,
      might they have wondered about and thought about?
P: The sun.

This moving between subjects was not idle chatter. What the teacher was doing by careful intervention was enabling the pupils to address difficult questions, in the same way as did the Gold Class teacher. The teacher frequently offered feedback in doing so, nominated pupils and used assisting questions – and a high number of these questions were discursive. This kind of talk moves the lesson towards dialogue and offers the possibility that the pupils have as much, or even more, expertise than the teacher. Associated with all of this is a remarkable frequency of lengthy pupil utterances. Let's have a look at what happened in a little more detail.

Here is an example from the lesson. The children's talk focuses on the controversial and difficult question of what happens after death. This is probably one of the oldest religious questions in the world. What is significant here is that it is the pupils who advance and debate the ideas. In our experience, regardless of what the teacher wants to talk about, questions of life and death are frequently raised by pupils. Here the teacher lets them do this.

A: Erm ... my my Mum thinks that when you die, your body goes away and your soul stays, erm, around.

T: Ah ... now Alice said something interesting there. Your soul. Right, now, let's just think about that for a second ... all of you just look this way a minute. Where is your soul? Now you can ... somebody's dead you can dissect the body do something called an autopsy and you can see all their organs ... their brain, their bones, everything, but where is your soul? It's nice to think we have got a soul, isn't it? It's nice to think cause we're human ... What is your soul? Where is it? What does it mean? What do you think, Sally?

> **Activity**
> Read John Burningham's book *Granpa* (1984) or E. B. White's *Charlotte's Web* (1981) or Susan Varley's *Badger's Parting Gifts* (1984). Compare how the book deals with death with how the children talk about it in the extract below.
>
> Compare the talk of these children and the talk of children you have encountered.

And a little later a pupil engaged in a similar way. This pupil used uptake with a peer. Uptake, as we have said, is rarely used by teachers and it is even rarer pupil-to-pupil.

P: Erm ... Is it like Leo Thatch said, is it like your body is just like a shell and inside it's like your spirit and stuff, and like you leave your body so you're the same but you don't have a body, like, cause you're dead?

T: That's a good way of putting it, I think, that's what a lot of people believe. It's very hard, isn't it, to say what a spirit or soul is cause you can't touch it, can you? You can only sort of feel it or sense it, you can't actually touch it, right Jon?

J: A ... it's like there's ... There's a TV advert with an Alka Seltzer inside.

T: Ahhh?

J: You see the inner self.

T: I think that's a very good way of putting it, Jon. Yeah, your inner self is your
   soul. I think that's a very good way of putting it. Nick?

The pupil talk draws on a range of knowledge but they make specific use of
common cultural knowledge. They use the advertisement to make explicit the
difficult concept they are dealing with. This use of a media metaphor and the
accompanying analogical argument is rare in most lessons. Hay *et al.* (1996) also
claim that children use analogies drawn from contemporary media to help them
explicate difficult concepts when they are discussing spirituality.

Main faith traditions

Bronze Class

It is Tuesday afternoon. A Year 3 class is sitting in their classroom. Their male
teacher begins the lesson by telling the children the story of Abraham and Isaac.
It is a problematic story for such young children. The teacher does not simply tell
the story, he ensures that the children attend by asking them pertinent questions.
These questions do more than check attention to the task. They skilfully guide
the children to empathise with the characters by seeking their views on Abraham's
feelings at key changes in the narrative. The children are then set the tasks of
retelling the story in small groups and identifying questions they would like to ask
Abraham. At the end of the lesson, they use these questions in a hot-seat activity
and in doing discover a good deal about how to empathise and thus to understand
difficult and complex situations. In this case, the framing of the lesson is relatively
stronger than those above, in that the teacher has had to plan so that the discussion
leads relatively seamlessly into the drama, hot-seating activity.

In this lesson, the teacher engages in quite a high proportion of management
talk: telling the pupils to get into groups, explaining the group tasks and finally
setting up the hot-seat activity. Even so, there was a low percentage of checking
questions and statements but a relatively high percentage of discursive talk, with
ninety-seven discursive statements produced during this lesson. The frequency of
the use of these utterances is not simply a matter of raw percentages but of lengthy
sequences of them. In this case, because the pupils were engaged in peer questioning, they produced more discursive utterances than was invited by the teacher's
prompts. For instance, a pupil (P) nominated Emma (E) as a speaker and Emma's
question invited discursive talk:

E: What did Sarah ask you when you got home?

P: 'What were you doing?'

T: And what did you say to that question?

P: (*Nominates another speaker.*)
P: How did you feel when you had to sacrifice Isaac?
P: Very sad indeed.
  (*A little later ...*)
T: Socrates, have you got a question?
S: Yeah, when the killing that (*gestures throat slit*). Why? – Because you not
   happy for it.
T: (*Paraphrases.*)
P: Er em, because, er em, because God told me to do it there.

This high proportion of peer questioning related to thoughts and feelings encourages the exploration of meaning. This exploration can only come about through engagement which requires the use of discursive talk.

Orange Class

The children are in their own classroom. It is a Year 5 class. The teacher begins the lesson by inviting the children to talk about their work on 'backgrounds' in art, an activity they have done in art. The children do not understand the relevance of this at all, so she rapidly tells them what is going to happen; she makes the up-and-coming task explicit. An enlarged text is introduced. The text is about key questions raised by different faith traditions. She then goes on to say that today they will be discussing Buddhism. The class is divided into four groups and each group is set the task of discussing a range of materials related to the faith of Buddhism.

This lesson, like the one above, draws extensively on peer-to-peer talk. The lesson was more strongly classified than many of lessons discussed in this chapter, only because the teacher was explicit about the religion under consideration, and the nature of the task they were to undertake: looking for evidence of what Buddhism might be about. The pupils engaged with the task with enthusiasm and supported each other as they explored the task; two-thirds of the talk was on task. The teacher's talk was less discursive than that of the pupils, although 38 per cent of her utterances were assisting questions. The pupils often went beyond what the teacher demanded. We can relate this to the way the teacher modelled cognitive talk for the pupils and also structured the discourse as a model. The type and quantity of the pupils' talk is related to the careful management and organisation of the groups and the work set for them. Given the comparatively tighter classification and framing than in the other religious education lessons we have seen, it is of interest to note the pupils 'thinking aloud' in responding to the task. These thoughts were comparatively sophisticated and reveal pupils trying to make meaning and gain understanding. An example demonstrates this:

P: Em, Buddha isn't really a god/ It's just, he's somebody that should em. He
   shows a right life for everyone.

T: Say it again, in a really big voice. So we can all hear it. (*this spoken more loudly*)

P: I think that Buddha isn't really a god. He is just someone who thought that people shouldn't be and they should do things like / not telling a lie and not hurting anybody.

The sophistication is clear; this pupil recognises that, commonly, it is thought that Buddha is one of many gods, but for this pupil, Buddha is understood not as a god but as a guide, 'showing the way, illuminating the path'.

A further example of prioritising pupils' thinking comes a little later. The teacher has asked about what is important to Buddhists.

P: I think nature is important to them because they had, erm, pictures, of erm the erm, those eels.

T: Sorry/little bit louder.

P: I think nature's important to them because they are releasing eels into the sea.

This resonates with another Year 5 lesson we have not discussed in detail in this book. The teacher asked what life was for and the pupils responded:

P1: Because, err, if we weren't here, there won't be many people to look after the world/ I think

P2: To look after the world, you could learn, like/ you could help people learn to look after things/ cos, like, anybody looks after things/ like pollute and everything.

We believe that these little discourses make the points that pupils are keen to discuss their moral concern about environmental matters, and that the nature of talk in religious education sessions creates space for them to do this.

Lessons to be learnt

We are now in a position to illustrate what good teachers of religious education do in whole class situations. They prioritise opportunities for discursive talk and avoid closed questions. They minimise the use of checking questions, which ensures that pupils do not feel they have to find the one right answer. They tend to use weaker framing than in other subject areas, such as English or mathematics. Most importantly, they accept the pupils' ideas and comments in a non-judgmental manner and this can only come about because the framing is weak.

When teaching about main faith traditions, they employ a limited range of learning outcomes, use a story and organise group work. They promote cognitively orientated talk and make this clear (visible) to the pupils. They give the pupils space to engage in sustained talk and enable them to risk thinking out loud.

In the case of puzzling questions, they recognise that dealing with such questions involves a variable range of learning outcomes. We could say that engaging the pupils in the task means that they cannot always specify in advance where the talk will lead and therefore which learning outcomes will be visited. Teachers promote cognitively orientated talk, but in these sessions they have to work harder to make the focus clear (visible) to the children. As with main faith traditions, they allow opportunity for sustained talk and thus the children demonstrate that they can reach beyond national expectations.

Chapter 7

Checking learning and engagement and opening a dialogue in mathematics

In this chapter, you will see how teachers:

- use careful questions to keep pupils on task and to check previous learning
- use checking questions as a form of rapid assessment
- enable pupils to explore mathematics through their own talk
- who work with mixed-age classes can provide differentiation through whole talk discourse.

Mathematics is not merely a core subject of the National Curriculum but, like reading, is a subject that creates high states of public anxiety. The general public, the popular press, some public figures and some politicians never tire of telling us that children can no longer do arithmetic accurately. The stated aim of the policy introducing the *Numeracy Strategy* and its successor, the *Primary National Strategy*, was to raise the achievement of pupils in mathematics and, in 2007, the Minister responsible claimed that this goal had been reached: 'Mathematics has risen for the fourth year in a row by one percentage point to 77 per cent, with improvements for both boys and girls' (DfCSF Press Notice 2007/0145).

The agenda for the teaching of mathematics in recent years, certainly since the introduction of the strategy, has focused on the manipulation of numbers – particularly the mental manipulation of numbers. Some commentators have noted that children's entitlement to mathematics has been eroded because of this focus on particular and assessable aspects of numeracy. For much of the teaching time in many schools, arithmetic rather than mathematics is addressed, with less time being spent, for instance, on geometry.

Recent research and reviews of the *National Numeracy Strategy* point to the difficulty in ensuring that all pupils study all of the mathematics programme in the National Curriculum. Those aspects of the programme which require more open-ended thinking and problem-solving by pupils are the ones which seem to suffer most neglect. Raiker (2002), drawing on her own data, claims that the strategy does not allow pupils to articulate their own thinking and concerns in mathematics. Others argue that the daily lessons are characterised by an emphasis on teacher direction, closed questions and choral responses (Smith *et al.* 2004).

Speedy exchanges are often the driving force of the pedagogical strategy of the daily lesson. It is not unusual for speedy responses to be confused with pace. What this is about is the momentum of the lesson. The rapidity of verbal exchanges should not be confused with movement across learning outcomes, which to some extent is what pace is about (cf Alexander 2000). The original *Numeracy Strategy* document shares this confusion: 'in the first part of the lesson you get off to a clear start and maintain a brisk pace' (DfEE 1999: 13). Alexander (2000) is helpful here, in that his descriptions and definitions enable us to understand that pace not about momentum alone. He defines the concept of pace as having five aspects:

- organisational pace – the speed at which lesson preparations, introductions, transitions and conclusions are handled
- task pace – the speed at which learning tasks and their contingent activities are undertaken
- interactive pace – the pace of teacher–pupil and pupil–pupil exchanges, and contingent factors such as maintaining focus, and the handling of cues and turns
- cognitive or semantic pace – the speed at which conceptual ground is covered in classroom interaction, or the ratio of new material to old and of task demand to task outcome
- learning pace – how fast pupils actually learn. (Alexander 2000: 424)

The examples of teaching that we offer throughout this book demonstrate that skilled teachers have at least an intuitive understanding of the complexity of pace. This is very important in the teaching of mathematics, where speed has been prioritised by the authors of the *National Numeracy Strategy* and other policy-makers and commentators. As a consequence, they present interactive pace as being more significant than cognitive or semantic pace. For example, in the first sixty-one utterances in Green Class (see below), all focus on the task and cover just one learning outcome. So although there is rapidity about the lesson, the cognitive pace here is relatively slow. This is important because the teacher is responsive to the needs of the class; she recognises that some pupils need more time to learn the same material.

Activity

What does the *National Numeracy Strategy* say teachers should do during the daily mathematics lesson?

How much time should be spent on each section?

Compare what the strategy document advises with what you observe in your class.

What does this say to you about pace?

The daily mathematics lesson

Unlike the original *Literacy Strategy*, the *Numeracy Strategy* was less wedded to the clock; its recommended lesson length was forty-five to sixty minutes. In the original documentation, the structure of the lesson is in three parts:

- oral work and mental calculation
- the main teaching activity
- a plenary.

The first activity, it says, should occupy five to ten minutes; the second, thirty to forty minutes; and the plenary, ten to fifteen minutes. The main teaching activity is described as 'teacher input and pupil activities'; in the classes we have studied, both the first oral/mental work and the teaching component of the main activity have been whole class activities.

In the context of this structure, let's examine how skilled teachers are able to address the learning needs and demands of a wide variety of pupils in whole class sessions. Nowhere is this challenge more apparent than in mixed-age classes in rural schools. Let's look in detail at what happens in two such classes. The Standard Attainment Tests (SATs hereafter) results in these two classes show the relevant age groups achieving above national expectations. For both classes, our analysis and description focus on the whole class components of the first two parts of the daily lesson. Our teachers are confident and so treat the structure set out in the document flexibly, always bearing in mind the needs of the class and its pupil groups.

Green Class

This class is taught by a woman with the support of a learning assistant. There are eleven boys and four girls from Year 2, and eight boys and four girls from Year 3. Like many classes in rural areas, primary class size is maintained by combining two year groups – a typical organisational strategy in such schools and one regularly employed in smaller urban schools. There are three children described as having special educational needs.

It is Wednesday morning and, after registration, the children are sitting on the carpet. The teacher begins with quick mental calculations. Children are asked to engage in tasks related to the ordering of whole numbers up to 1,000 and addition and subtraction of factors up to twenty. This is conducted with great rapidity. It is followed by the main teaching activity, the theme of which is suitable units for measuring, which will lead to practical measuring later.

In the first part of the lesson, the pupils respond to the teacher's utterances and in doing so use a very high number of short utterances (three words or less). Sixty-one utterances used by the teacher and the pupils were related to the theme of the first part of the lesson, the ordering of whole numbers. Twenty-six of these were pupil utterances, of which twenty-one were of three words or less. Only one learning outcome is visited for this activity and virtually all the utterances were on task. You may recall from the two previous chapters that lessons there followed a different pattern. Here this part of the lesson was characterised by speed, with the teacher employing 'What do pupils know?' questions to check pupils' knowledge from previous lessons and engagement with the current lesson focus. There was a very high level of pupil nomination. These nominations all used the same question form, and substantive use of the kind of question 'Guess what teacher is thinking?' was also employed. The teacher is able to keep up the rapidity or momentum of the lesson because of the fact that she knows what the pupils know and uses that knowledge in the distribution of the questions. The target age group for these questions was Year 2 pupils rather than fully including the Year 3 pupils as well; only seven questions were addressed to Year 3 pupils. It is only when ordering numbers that girls were nominated to answer 'guess what teacher is thinking' questions.

Here is an example from the class. The teacher has a sequence of numbers written on the board; she is essentially dealing with size order.

T: Ninety-seven would be the largest one, right. I have done that one. So which one would be the next one, the next largest number? Lillian?

L: Eighty-three.

T: That would be eighty-three, wouldn't it? Yeah, have you noticed I left a space?

P: Yeah.

T: What would have happened if I'd written eighty-three there?

P1: Nine hundred and seventy eighty.

P2: Nine thousand.

T: It would make nine thousand.

P: Nine thousand seven hundred and eighty-three.

T: Yes, it would change that number completely, so you leave a space, please, to show me it's a new number. Right, which would be the next number? We are going in order now, which will be next? Kylie?

Here we can see the teacher using checking questions but she does more than that. She blends the checking questions with careful modelling of how to write numbers in sequence. She uses questions both to check that the children can sequence and that they have followed her model of the writing process. This careful use of language accompanied by practical demonstration means that she is also able to check the quality of her own instructional utterances and the development of pupil understanding through the pupils' responses; she gets the right answers from the pupils she nominates.

A similarly brisk approach is adopted when the second learning outcome is visited, with the addition and subtraction of factors up to twenty. During this part of the lesson, the Year 3 pupils were more involved. It is during this part of the lesson that the teacher begins to ask the older children discursive questions. In this part, a limited number of opportunities for discursive talk are provided but, when they are, the children always respond in kind. The teacher's approach to differentiation now demonstrates an interplay between subject knowledge and discursive questioning focused on the Year 3 pupils. Here the interactive pace slows down, partly because the pupil utterances are longer, more hesitant and thoughtful.

P: Miss Cab, I think it's going up. (*Looking at the results of subtraction from ten.*)
T: (*Laughs.*) Have you spotted a pattern? Well done, good girl.
P: Makes it down the side. (*Referring to the number pattern.*)
T: Oh, it makes it easier, doesn't it Catherine/ when you have spotted a
    pattern?

Catherine is a pupil defined as having special educational needs. We can see here the teacher involving her in a discursive manner. Her approach to Catherine reflects her approach to teaching mathematics; the teacher uses a sophisticated procedure that differentiates by age, need and learning outcome expectations.

Activity
Observe the first part of the daily mathematical lesson and note who is nominated, then note how they are categorised by gender and special needs.

If you are in a mixed-age class, make similar notes with respect to age.

Discuss your observations with the teacher.

You might want to ask why certain pupils were nominated.

The theme of the lesson now turned to simple units of measure. The children are encouraged to pass around a variety of parcels. These parcels are of varying volumes and mass, such that it is not possible by sight alone to say which is heavier. During this, the children are asked to guess/speculate on which parcel is heaviest, which they do. After a short while a kilogram weight is introduced and similarly passed around. At this point the teacher emphasises the need for care, uses contingency management. She does not allow pupils to engage in a discussion of what might happen but proceeds with the focus of the lesson. Before the utterance below, the pupils discussed what might happen if they dropped or were careless with the weight. She does not allow pupils to engage in discussion of what might happen but proceeds with the focus of the lesson.

T: Yes, so if we are holding one of these we hold it in front of us and then we
    can use both hands. Certainly not lifting it up high.

P: Yeah, cause then.

T: So a kilogram then. Well, what do you think then? Do you think it was /
  quite heavy or quite light?

P: Quite light.

P: Quite light.

P: Heavy.

P: Light.

P: Light.

T: Quite heavy / I think it's quite heavy. I think that's

P: Light.

The extract is clearly discursive in that the pupils confidently contribute to the discussion. We can also see how skilfully the teacher maintains the focus by refusing to be drawn into speculating as to what might happen if the weight were mishandled. She also gently refuses to accept the judgement that the kilogram weight is light in comparison to the other objects. She then asks the children to say how many 'Lacey bricks' make up a kilogram, thus quietly integrating the use of a standard measure into the lesson. The children's first guesses are very inaccurate; they consistently underestimate the weight of the combined 'Lacey bricks'. The focus age group for this activity is the Year 2 pupils. In her questioning, the teacher focuses on the correct use of language. It is the language of mathematical description and explanation that is being sought. Twenty-two utterances after the extract above, the teacher returns to the question of heaviness.

T: That was me doing that, William – (*moving the balance*) – we've got eight of
  those then and it still hasn't moved at all, let it alone for a minute, Abel. It
  hasn't moved at all. So a kilogram is quite a heavy weight then, isn't it?

Girls and boys are equally involved as nominated speakers, even though the gender distribution does not merit that. This part of the lesson contains a very high volume of on-task talk by both teacher and pupils. Learning outcomes are visited sequentially and there is no overlapping evident. Now the lesson proceeds: in the section below, we can see how she models the nature of the task through nomination of the younger pupils. She then makes it explicit to the pupils that this is what they will be doing. As you will notice, the pupils are confident that it is a matter for discussion.

T: Now I don't even know if I can get enough stuff for the bucket to balance
  the kilogram. We'll then add a few more then. That's three of them, four
  of them. Thank you, let's try the fat ones first. Can they all fit in? Has it
  moved at all, this one?

P: No.

T: How many have you got there now, Adam?

P: Six.

T: Six of these fat ones. Try that one.

P: (*Cross-talk one second.*)

T: Move at all. No, let's try the big fat one // I don't know if we can fit many more in, actually.

P: It doesn't

T: Well look. That was me doing that, Noel. We've got eight of those then and it still hasn't moved at all. Let it alone for a minute, Abel. It hasn't moved at all. So my ... So a kilogram is really quite a heavy weight then, isn't it?

P: If you dig out.

T: Now, in a minute we are going to be splitting into our groups and we are going to see if we can find some things that are, weigh the same as, a kilogram or less than a kilogram or about the same. Which is this then? Which of these were

P: Less.

T: They were a

P: A lot less.

T: They were a lot less than a kilogram. They didn't even make it come at all, did they, did they? So, and I've filled up the bucket. I can't put anything else in there now.

P: Yes, you can. Look.

Although the teacher occupies the largest percentage of talking time, what she does is open up the possibilities of the task and enables the pupils to engage in a dialogue. They are confident that they can argue a case and challenge the teacher. The result of this is that the pupils understand what they have to do but the task is open ended; she has put them in a position where they have to think.

The use of nomination indicates the degree to which this teacher is skilled in dealing not merely with a mixed-ability class but also one which has mixed ages in the same class. The distribution of nominations is such that the youngest are drawn in at the beginning and in the practical activity. The distribution between boys and girls reflects the composition of the class.

Red Class

This class is taught by a man and has six boys and four girls from Year 5, and twelve boys and eleven girls from Year 6, again a mixed-age class. There are no children on the school's register of special educational needs in this class. It is Wednesday after playtime. The room is set out in two parallel rows, across the width of the room, facing the whiteboard (front). The children are sitting at the desks in the rows.

The content or focus of the lesson as established by the teacher at the beginning of the lesson is decimal notation. The teacher begins by quickly checking the pupils' skill in sequencing numbers involving decimals. On the whiteboard he has written decimal numbers in random order and he asks them to sequence them one number at a time. They respond by writing on their personal whiteboards and then holding them up. The teacher routinely acknowledges that pupils have completed the task by naming them. This introduction proceeds with speed. He then asks named pupils to come and write the answers on the large whiteboard. Typically:

T: Lucia, come and put the next number up. (*She writes on the board.*) Thank you – Is she right?

The pupils confirm the accuracy of Lucia's answer. There is then a seamless move into the substantive content of the lesson. This part focuses on the same learning outcome as the beginning of the lesson.

During the whole class interaction for this lesson this teacher asked twenty-six questions; eighteen were assessment questions that monitored and checked pupils' current progress. These questions were almost invariably followed by feedback and individual pupils were nominated as recipients and/or speakers. The majority of these verbal interactions focused on the learning objective: decimal notation up to three places. The teacher issued a lot of instructions about what the children were to do and modelled what was to be done on eleven occasions. Five of the modelling incidents were psycho-motor in type, involving the teacher writing and erasing numbers on the whiteboard. In addition, he modelled the cognitive activity on six occasions. This sort of modelling involved the teacher showing how he analysed and thought about the problem, in essence here stressing the significance of the decimal point and its position in relationship to the numbers.

T: Who can tell me the next one? (*i.e. in the decimal sequence*) / Who can tell me the next one, Veronica?
V: Two point one.
T: Two point one, Veronica, that's a good try but we've got two numbers left. Which do you think is the smallest out of those two, Veronica? Two or two point one?
V: Two.
T: You sure? Cos two point one is two and a little bit more, isn't it? So number two must be … Tell you what, Veronica, do want to come and write the number two for us? / See if you can come and write where it goes.

Another feature of the teacher discourse is the use of statements that are offering cognitive structuring to the pupils. In this case, he shows pupils how to do the problem, in essence how to sequence the numbers. You could see this as a sort of 'thinking out loud' process. The teacher was telling the pupils what to do, showing them what to do and explaining how things are done. The use of checking questions enables him to confirm that the pupils are following the lesson and are developing an understanding of the topic. This is an effective and efficient sequence – an example of good teaching – but it is unsurprising. What might be surprising is that a pupil was able to introduce a new learning objective, not merely for himself but for other pupils.

P: Sir, we decided to add them all up.

T: Good, you can tell me the answer in a minute – a little challenge for the boys over there, just to add them all. Er right / next one, Helga.

H: I put one point zero one.

T: One point zero one, good, so I'm going to cross them off. Well, first of all we know these are the smallest because they begin with zeros. We've worked out which is the ... We've done that one. Right, next one, Richard.

R: One point 'o' six.

T: Try and say 'zero' instead of 'o', so 'zero' – and 'o' is a letter. Try and get into the habit of that. Good, Nicole.

What is happening is that the teacher is accepting the pupils' ideas and using them – a very good example of what Martin Nystrand (in Nystrand *et al.* 1997) has called 'uptake'. This does not mean that the teacher takes up the theme immediately; he returns to it later. He does this in order to return to the younger pupils. As we will show you, this is a very bold bit of teaching because the teacher does not know the answer to the problem specified by the pupils and therefore the question and answer can be said to be authentic. Most often, teachers know the answers in mathematics and ask only that pupils display their knowledge. These are the kind of questions that may be coded as 'Guess what's in my head?' or 'What do pupils know?' Some researchers call these kinds of questions 'requests for display'– with 'display' meaning to show or display your knowledge. There is powerful descriptive evidence from a variety of sources that the classroom discourse of mathematics teaching is largely composed of requests for display. What we have tried to show you is how these are woven into the mathematics lesson, enabling the teacher to know what pupils know and use that to inform the ongoing lesson.

After this brief interjection and the teacher's uptake of the pupils' suggestion, the teacher returns to main theme of the lesson. The discourse employed, as we said above, is instructional and most of the questions are checking questions. He is explaining and assuring himself that the pupils are following the theme. It is clear that the lesson he planned would have proceeded along these lines, closely following the learning objective. But the interjection means he has had to adapt his teaching strategy, since he wanted to enable the pupils to engage with their own ideas and problems. It must be noted that what the pupils proposed was a learning objective commensurate with the *Numeracy Strategy*'s Year 6 programme. In fact, they were progressing the topic more rapidly than either the teacher expected or the strategy document specifies. What they have done is to change the pace of the lesson; it is not simply a matter of speed but of the development of conceptual understanding.

Activity

Here are two scenarios:

1. During a lesson on the equivalence of fractions, three Year 4 pupils suggest that even though ⅛ equals ¼ they are not the same, because if you divide a cake in this way bits will be lost. Are they are treating the question as a matter of sharing rather than division? Do you change the lesson to follow up this observation? If you do, what will the lesson look like?

2. During a lesson on the naming of flat shapes in a Reception class, two pupils ask if can they fit the shapes together to make a picture. They are being asked simply to label the shapes. Would you change the lesson plan?

What learning objective(s) would they then be following, and what would the lesson look like?

Towards the end of the whole class interactive segment, our teacher returns to the group attempting to add the decimal numbers. He wants to know what they have achieved but, equally importantly, he needs to know that they understand the content all the class have followed and the content they have set themselves. He incorporates the group back into the mainstream and asks them to give an account of what they have done. They respond by saying what they made the addition totals to be. The pupils engage in a genuine conversation from which he is excluded, since he does not know the answer, not having tackled or set the problem. This brief extract is an example of highly skilled teaching, which you should look at carefully. Think how it might be a model for your own teaching of mathematics.

T: Right, John and John, what did you make the total?
J1: Er, sixty-eight, wasn't it?
J2: I made it …
T: Sixty-eight?
J2: I've been thinking that it's six point eighty-eight.
M: Yeah, that's what I made it.
S: Oh yeah.
T: Six point eight eight. And what do you think it is John?
C: He thinks it's
J1: I got sixty-eight but
T: Well, I'll you it must if if this is
W: Seven point nine six.

T: Easy way to check. How many ones have you got? – one, two, three, four,
     five, six – it must be six point eight eight, alright. Count the six.
JI: Because we put the noughts in and added it all together but we've put the
     point in the wrong place.

We can see here how the teacher enables the pupils to be discursive by letting
them talk to each other and by avoiding telling them what they mean. He does not
give a definitive answer to their problem; he doesn't know the problem until they
explain it to him. He realises that the pupils need new information and proceeds
to model mathematical methods of approximation, which will enable the pupils
to identify their own errors. The pupils go beyond this and offer an explanation
of how the error arose by exposing their thinking. The teacher then rehearsed
the main learning outcomes one more time and then set the pupils to work on
identified tasks. The lesson comes full circle.

Lessons to be learnt

What is very clear from Green Class and also from Red Class is the way in which
teachers are confident in their knowledge of what pupils know. How do they
get this knowledge? What they are looking for in our examples is the knowledge
pupils are using in the class at that time; in the case of mathematics, as much
knowing how to do a problem as knowing an arithmetical fact. Both teachers use
checking questions in a very careful manner. It is easy to ask the pupils who we are
certain will give us the right answers, but in this case we can see teachers asking
boys and girls across age groups so that the widest range of pupils are involved.
The checking questions are carefully formulated and stick closely to the learning
objective that is being taught. This business of knowing what they know also
means that pupils are not publicly embarrassed by their lack of knowledge. So you
can see that proper checking questions in the hands of skilled teacher are part of
the teaching in the lesson and not merely tests.

The sequence of the lesson is interesting. In both cases the learning objectives
are differentiated and, at the beginning, the younger pupils are nominated to
answer questions that are at their level of challenge; older pupils are drawn in
more towards the middle of the lesson and are asked more challenging questions.
At the end of a lesson sequence, the questioning returns to the younger and the
learning objectives are reiterated for all pupils. Involvement comes about from
both the questioning and the instruction. What is noticeable is the relative absence
of questions used as disciplinary devices or of simple management utterances
related to behaviour.

There are three important things to note. First, a very large proportion of the
talk by both pupils and teachers is on task. The lessons proceed at a brisk rate
and can do so because the learning objectives are carefully articulated so that the
topic covered is in the minds of all participants, including the teacher. Second,
the themes are simple but are adhered to throughout the sequence. Knowledge is

strongly classified, except in the case of the boys who choose to try the addition of decimals – even so, the learning objective they move to is closely related to the one in hand. Third, the framing of the lessons is consistently tight. A common feature of both classes is that both pupils and teachers address one learning outcome at a time; this may be a peculiarity of mathematics. It sometimes might be thought that tight framing rules out discursive teaching but, we would argue, in the case of Red Class, that it enables the use of discursive talk rather than impedes it. In Green Class a similar relationship can be observed and some pupils maintain discursive talk without teacher intervention. We shall return to this at the end of the book.

Chapter 8

Pupils saying what they think and clarifying their meanings using contemporary communications technology

In this chapter, you will learn about:

- a broad view of contemporary communications media
- reflection on changing technologies and digital inclusion
- pupils learning to use equipment and software
- teachers using equipment and software
- conversations that demand pupils' accounts of their media experience.

Until the late 1990s television played a significant role in schools, for example almost all primary school children watched *Words and Pictures* and *Look and Read* as part of their reading lessons. You can probably remember sitting and watching these and other programmes yourself. The common practice was for the whole class to sit in front of the screen and watch the broadcast live, until video recorders became cheap and common. But the last twenty years or so have seen a revolution in the use of communication technology in schools. It's sometimes easy to forget how rapidly new technology has been introduced into schools. Just thirty years ago schools made occasional use of a cine projector, usually a treat at Christmas, and some teachers used slides and film strips and others made use of tape recorders. The first wave of new technology to come into primary schools included the specially designed and produced BBC micro-computers; each primary school was given one machine and the software was on an audio tape. Specially designed machines became more sophisticated and a range of machines – usually incompatible with each other – were used in schools. If you go into any primary school now, you will encounter a range of sophisticated hardware and software. What you will also notice is that, though software is specifically designed for schools, the hardware is more or less the same as that used in commerce, industry and the home. What you will also notice is how many children talk about using their home computer and the way in which teachers sometimes suggest that children use the home machine to search the World Wide Web.

We can't ignore the debate that has gone on around the use of technologies in teaching. First radio then television were seen as the 'enemies' of educational development; particularly, it was said that their use would undermine the need to read. This kind of thinking can be described as a 'moral panic', in that those who propose it aren't relying on evidence but rather they offer an emotive opinion. There is a similar concern about the World Wide Web. If children are asked to use it in the privacy of their homes, will they access improper things? Will schools be encouraging the children to access illicit material? This has led schools to place 'internet filters' or 'content blockers' on their school systems in order to protect the children. This has sometimes had some interesting, unexpected consequences – for example, children can have difficulty looking for information on the 'blue tit' even though the Royal Society for the Protection of Birds website is pristine. Of more concern to some schools and teachers is what is termed the 'digital divide'. This refers to the fact that some pupils have access to computers and associated technologies and some do not. An independent study conducted for British Telecom (BT) identified two factors leading to digital exclusion:

- problems of access often associated with income and ability to pay for technology (home computing and internet access) but also issues such as disability and skills gaps
- problems of engagement whereby people do not see the need to engage with new technology and do not perceive the benefits of the online world.

(The Digital Divide in 2025:
An Independent Study Conducted for BT 2004)

It is the first of these factors that causes concern for teachers, because by asking the children to use home-based technology, they may be disadvantaging the poorest children. At a broader level, school differences may be exacerbated by the digital divide as a feature of wealth distribution. BT's future projection suggests that engagement may be more important but, of course, some families by then will have a long history of use and others little or no history of use. Children's digital access will continue to be a matter of professional concern, both in terms of access to appropriate materials and in terms of future opportunities to engage easily with developing technologies.

It would be a mistake to assume that communication technology is only about computers and their adjuncts, such as interactive whiteboards. The National Curriculum makes clear that the field is much broader and encompasses the use of audio-visual materials such as television, video recording, DVDs and audio recorders. In the substantive part of this chapter, we will deal with the wide range of technologies used in primary schools. Many of these technologies lend themselves best to individual/paired work, small group work and whole class discussion of the finished product and the process by which it was made. Such technologies have, of course, been used for straightforward instructional purposes, but best practice shows that it is the use of the technologies by children that is most valuable. These technologies follow a narrative form but allow those narratives to be stored, replayed and revised. The recording/storing of information is not 'visible' to the children; they record and replay later. We make this point because, presently, we will discuss in detail the use of the interactive whiteboard – a technology that seems to us to have radically different possibilities and will perhaps produce differences in pedagogy.

Lorac and Weiss's (1981) groundbreaking book on the use of the widest range of audio-visual materials available at that time argued that using those materials developed communication and social skills. These authors also demonstrated that pupils learnt concepts and information by making multi-media materials. The National Curriculum specifies that the widest range of technologies be studied and used. The English subject orders for Key Stages 1 and 2 require that pupils record, listen to and watch their own recordings, as well as studying published materials. For instance, in the case of reading there is the specific requirement to read and analyse ICT-based information texts, while for writing pupils should 'assemble and develop ideas on paper and on screen'. You will also find that the subject orders in mathematics, geography, art and design, and music, for instance, all require the use of ICT; in fact, every subject of the curriculum except physical education does this. In the design of the original National Curriculum and its revision in 1995, ICT was not a statutory subject. The revision of the National Curriculum in 2000 made it statutory, and it is required in all schools and all pupils have had an entitlement to it. This is a change that reflects the importance placed on its use by educators and policy-makers in the years since 1988.

Pupils learning to use equipment

In order to be able to know and understand audio-visual and other technologies, pupils need to be confident in how to use the machinery.

P: We don't know how to use it, cos we're nervous with it and
T: What about?
P: If you put everything on and tell us what to do, we could do it ourselves.
T: Alright, let's see if this works. Let's see if I can do what you told me to do.
    What have I got to do first?

This Year 3 class was at the beginning of learning how to use a video camera. The teacher has introduced the camera and said what the task would be. As you can see, the pupils feel empowered to express their concerns and then to suggest teaching strategies. How does the teacher teach the whole class to use a scarce resource? What happens is that individual pupils are instructed and then instructed to instruct their peers. The teacher hands over the instructional discourse to the pupils but is able to observe, check and intervene where necessary. This provides the teacher with an assessment opportunity and pupils with an opportunity to learn from each other.

While it is possible to introduce children to the use of equipment as a whole class, if they are quickly to become competent and confident users they need hands-on experience. It is more effective to set up learning to use equipment by putting the pupils to work in small groups. A teacher doing this may well make use of a learning support assistant to assist the pupils while they are engaging with the task.

Activity

Look at this brief transcript from a Year 5 class.

What are they learning to use?

How is the teacher helping their learning?

P1: There.

P2: There's a bit of things.

T: Yes, we can cover these over. You want the tree there? / Now that is a bit thick, that paint brush. I don't know, what do you think?

P: (*Unison.*) Yeah.

T: A bit big really, isn't it? So you want get rid of that? / So undo that, just go 'edit undo' / up to 'edit' / take the arrow up onto 'edit', now pull down one to 'undo' / that first one, there.

P2: What did you do?

Our practical work has demonstrated that even the youngest pupils can become confident users of computers, video cameras, digital cameras, audio tape recorders and sophisticated and transparent software. They can then use them to make their own products. The range of activities that they can engage in when they become skilled operators is often quite remarkable. For example, the pupils in the exchange above quickly became confident users of photo editing software.

It is worth considering here how changes in technology now enable pupils to have easy access to processes which, in the past, were costly or time consuming or just very difficult. We argue that the best way to think about using new technologies is analogous to how we have argued for the use of talk. Pupils and teachers collaborate to make meaning through the use of a variety of technologies, so it is not simply a matter of taking a digital photograph or looking up a website. The use of new technologies produces changes in pedagogy. What is attractive to pupils and teachers is the immediacy that these technologies offer. Few will be surprised by the excitement generated when children email images of their activities on school camp.

Exchanging and modifying images

Exchanging messages between pupils in different schools requires that pupils know and understand the following:

1   how emails and their attachments can be sent and received
2   how those messages can be modified, and this includes any visual images
3   how language helps to give particular meanings to images.

One useful activity requires pupils to send an incomplete image of themselves, using email attachments but with no background, to their partners. The partners are invited to complete the image by providing the background. Sometimes a caption is provided by the sender, which makes the task more challenging since the image is less open to interpretation and reinterpretation. You might try this activity, but as you will know you may not reproduce the images, for reasons of safety and child protection.

We now turn to making the image and learning how language pins down the image rather precisely.

Children using digital imaging

P1: Yes and, erm, you took a picture of it and plugged it into the computer and it loaded up and your, erm, image came up.
P2: Come out on the computer.
P1: If it went wrong, you could just print the image out from the computer. And if it went wrong, you could run like something in the background you didn't want. You just took a different colour off the picture and you just placed it over the things, and then all the stuff you didn't want, you could change it.

This exchange shows how pupils use language to clarify what the technology can do. Effectively the first pupil is structuring the editing process for the second pupil who, in turn, is clarifying the discourse. The teacher is confident in allowing the pupils to use expensive resources to make their own sense and meanings of them. It is this confidence that enables the pupils to use talk in the way they do.

Here are children describing how they plan and take images. In doing this, they comment on what they think the final image will look like and establish criteria by which they will consider it to be successful.

P1: Yes, because her friend changed hers, because hers was looking forward, erm, forward to the court, and there were loads of cars and people everywhere and she didn't really want it. So she turned it around to the house by the, like sort of where the sort of hedgerow was, on the ground bit, so she had a more, erm, more interesting background than people walking past, like more.
P2: Yes, because it would get a bit confusing if you had some moving, other moving things in the background, as well.
P1: Yes.
P2: So you had to make sure there / if you had railings in the background, you

had to make sure there wasn't a car coming past, otherwise it would look a bit confusing, something whizzing past on the photograph.

P1: Yes, because I was going to have mine on here but around the other way, facing things, so you could see the actual cars in the road. And there were lots of cars parked and cars going down the road and it was bit busy that day, so I just took it round the other way and took it from there, so that you don't see the movement.

P2: And erm / mine never really turned out right, because er the / I had erm the first couple of attempts, the ball kept falling off the /

The first thing you have probably noticed is how long the utterances are, and you will also have noted that the teacher keeps quiet. You can see how the pupils build meaning by interacting with each other. They use examples to develop a structure of meaning that explains why backgrounds are important and the effect that changing the point of view has on the final meaning of an image. In short, they come to a principle by which they can judge the success of what they are doing. This kind of talk shows evidence of their thinking and is characterised by pauses and fillers as they struggle to make the principle explicit. The pupils are not being told what the principle is; they are being given space to develop it themselves. This requires the kind of talk that they use.

Here a Year 1 class is discussing the nature of images. Even though the children are so young, they are able to respond to questions about how an image is put together and what sorts of things make it meaningful. In the interaction between the children and the teacher, we can see that the children's utterances are often of the type 'Guess what teacher is thinking?', but the feedback provided takes their thinking on – or perhaps, more properly, we can see their thinking in the way they talk. The teacher has converted an overhead transparency into a jigsaw projected via an overhead projector. This resource enables the teacher to construct and reconstruct an image as the children comment.

T: One thing we need / to know that it was a footballer / what would that be?

P1: A football.

T: A football, good girl. So there's a football. (*Adds football to image.*) And there is a footballer. (*Adds caption 'Footballer' to image.*) Now / supposing I change that?

P2: 'Football girl.'

T: Supposing I change that, could I change that? (*Points at football.*)

P: (*Unison.*) Yes.

T: What else could I put on?

P3: A ball shaped like an egg.

T: A ball shaped like an egg?

P3: Yeah.

T: And if I put a ball shaped like an egg / what would they be playing then?

P4: Egg football.

P: (*Unison.*) Egg football.

P4: And when they kick the egg, it'll crack.

After joking about an egg ball, the pupils confirm that the image would become one of a rugby player. This mutual play with images engages them with the construction of image. And through the interaction, they are learning that the meaning of an image can be changed by manipulating it. They are learning that an image or images may have component parts that contribute to the total meaning. This knowledge forms the basis of any understanding of how visual communications media work.

Children as television critics

Inside and outside school, children are exposed to television on a daily basis. In school, it is nearly always what can be described as 'educational television' – programmes designed to impart particular knowledge. Outside school, the kinds of television they see is much more varied and will include realistic drama, comedy, cartoons and news – in fact, the range of programmes that you watch yourself. Children are able to identify the difference between educational television and the rest of television. Faced with a programme that looks like a drama but is in fact a history programme, they will say that it's educational because you watch it in school.

Even very young children are able to describe television programmes in terms that are generalisable; they categorise their viewing. Their own classifications do not always follow the distinctions made by adults. They make up their own categories, drawing on criteria they understand. For instance, they talk about programmes involving children as a category, even though many of those programmes belong to different genres. So a programme that is a drama with children in it is often categorised with a children's quiz programme. They are actively making sense of their viewing for themselves.

Activity

Ask your pupils what television programmes they watch and how they would describe them? Do they define 'educational television' in the way the children above did?

There has been much concern that children simply passively absorb television programmes in an uncritical manner. You will have read and heard comments that suggest that children, in simply absorbing television, will treat all progammes as real and will thus lose sight of the difference between reality and fiction. For instance, some commentators have said that children do not understand that cartoon violence is simply 'make believe', and that they will expect real life reactions to violence to ape the reactions in cartoons. It is proposed that when a cartoon character falls from a cliff and then gets up, the children will expect this to happen in real life. However, all the scientific studies of children and television show this not to be true. They also show that children do not simply passively sit in front of television and absorb it; they watch and do many other things. Perhaps the only time that children focus all of their attention on the screen is when they watch television in school.

Let us look at what they say about television – in this case, a cartoon. These Reception and Year 1 infants are talking about the television they watch and, in this episode, they talk about the cartoon *Bugs Bunny*. The role of the teacher is to use delicate and sensitive questioning so that the children are given the opportunity to develop a critical commentary.

T: Who's never seen Bugs Bunny? Well, you've all seen it somewhere then? Um, what kind of
P1: It's a cartoon.
P2: I love it.
T: A cartoon, is it? What's a cartoon then?
P3: It's when there's cartoon time and pictures, all different pictures.

What we can see is that the children easily identify the genre. The teacher makes their knowledge relevant to the classroom by establishing what can be spoken about. And later the teacher develops this.

T: Is Bugs Bunny real?
P: (*Unison.*) No, no.
P1: He's just// he's just been drawn/he's just been drawn/but um/they move him by string/ but you can't see the string on.
T: Oh, you can't see the string?
P: No.
T: So, he's a puppet?
P1: Yes.
T: Is he a puppet? What do you think?
P2: He's just? A man's underneath him.
T: Oh.
P2: He moves him underneath.
P3: Yes.
P4: No.
T: No? / Don't you think so?
P4: You can't get people under a cartoon character.

The teacher uses discursive questioning to draw out the pupils' common cultural knowledge. Again, this is not the kind of knowledge that is usually valued in classrooms; you may have encountered times when children were 'told off' for talking about cartoons. The children are able to say that Bugs Bunny is not real; he isn't going to be seen on a news programme nor will they see him in their street. They are able to speculate about how the representation of Bugs Bunny is produced. The teacher's gentle questioning enables pupils to challenge each other; it is the questioning that establishes a productive discourse.

Interactive whiteboards

Arguably one of the most exciting innovations in classroom technology has been the introduction of interactive whiteboards. They enable teachers to share and show things to the whole class that previously could only be done on a one-to-one basis.

Activity

Search for either internet or CD sources provided by the Department for Education and Skills (DfES) on learning and teaching using ICT. The example video clips should be analysed using the framework we have provided.

Note how many examples might offer more powerful learning opportunities if direct experience were provided.

Note the ways in which teachers use the whiteboard to challenge children to think.

This example is drawn from the Department for Education and Skills (2004) pack *Learning and Teaching Using ICT*. These Year 1 children have been working on the story of Cinderella. They have dramatised it and taken digital photographs of the drama. The teacher stands in front of the whiteboard with a small group of children who have acted the story. She then tells the whole class, who are sitting on the carpet, to look at the pictures on the whiteboard. She talks first to the actors and then to the whole class.

T: Shall we look at the picture? Nidan, can you tell everybody what's happening in the picture?
N: The ugly sisters are cross because Cinderella is not wash, not not cleaning the floor.
T: Good girl, how do think that made Cinderella feel, Sunil?
S: Sad.
T: Sad, good boy. How else do you think it makes her feel? Edil?
E: It makes her feel lonely.
T: Have a look at the picture. What made you think that?

P: Just the sisters, they're pointing at Cinderella.

T: They are, aren't they? Is that why she feels lonely?

P: (*Unison.*) Yeah.

T: Well done.

She begins in a typical teacher manner, by apparently offering the children the choice to refuse the activity – of course, they understand what she means. They must attend to the picture. Nidan goes beyond simply answering the question, interprets the picture and is praised for it. The teacher picks up the children's theme and asks about feelings and then seeks to discover how they are able to ascribe feelings to the characters. When she gets the response, 'Just the sisters, they're pointing at Cinderella', she goes on to model the use of the pronoun 'they'. This is a good example of how a teacher working in a multi-lingual classroom is constantly teaching the conventions and uses of English.

One of the real tests of new technology use is to ask what it enables us to do that we could not do previously. It is important to ask such a question because otherwise ICT becomes just another gimmick, a piece of equipment to dazzle the children for a brief period of time. Unfortunately, some ICT use is like this. An excellent example of the use of ICT to do something we could not do previously is its use in some aspects of whole class science. There is a good example on the DfES materials. Here a teacher shares a microscope image with the whole class.

T: We are going to use this very fancy microscope linked to a computer. This we can put onto the board and also we are going to use the internet to research how we can ensure good hygiene to avoid illness. I've got a strawberry on a slide at the bottom, the microscope, and I'm going to put it into focus and we'll see what we can actually identify on this strawberry. You can tell me when you think it's focused ... right what can we identify on this strawberry? This strawberry is a day old. I've just taken it out of the garden ... What can we see, Liam?

L: White dots.

T: Which are there and there. What do think those white dots might be, Victoria?

V: Microorganisms.

T: They may well be microorganisms. What else might they be in a strawberry? Ashley?

A: Seeds.

The teacher begins by explaining what is to be done and describing the equipment. Without the special ICT apparatus, he would not be able to share the image of the strawberry with the class. Neither would he be able to engage them in speculation as to what the 'white dots' actually are. This is a very good example of how ICT can be used to teach whole classes in a way impossible in the past, because they are all sharing the same 'living' image. The teacher can also save images of the strawberry, showing how it changes over time.

Lessons to be learnt

ICT should not simply be some kind of attractive gizmo. It should enable us to do things better than we could do before; in a lot of cases, to do things we could not do in the past. (Think of the whiteboard and the microscope, for instance.) The best forms of talk around ICT are discursive, and the best uses of ICT are themselves discursive. ICT should be about children making and sharing meaning. This should remind us that ICT is more than simply using the latest computer technologies. It is worth noting that all of the examples we have used have involved lens-based media. Children readily engage with such media, although they may be nervous about it when they first use it. Much of what we have discussed involves children looking at parts of images, in order to produce informed judgements. In order to do this, the teacher is placed in the position of discussant rather than instructor. Instruction in necessary if the children are to use the equipment efficiently and effectively, but in order for the activity to be intellectually challenging, to be a way that children learn to think, then a subtle mix of the use of media and language is essential. In this case, it is anticipated that children will make sense of and with contemporary media. The teacher's job is to develop talk that challenges and clarifies meanings.

Chapter 9

From checking and instructing to predicting and describing – teaching science

In this chapter, you will learn:

- something of how the present science curriculum came about
- from examples how teachers move from instruction to challenging questions
- how pupils can be encouraged to use predictive language.

Science is the third core subject of the primary curriculum. It was one of the first subjects to be published when the National Curriculum orders came out in 1989. Unlike English and mathematics, it does not have a long history of being taught in primary school. In some form or another, English and mathematics have been taught since before 1870 but science really only became a core after the ERA 1988. From when we were at primary school, we remember not science but nature study. In our urban classroom, there was something called a nature table. On it there were objects such as acorns in autumn, and willow twigs in spring, and often a picture of red squirrel. We were introduced to the mystery of hibernation, usually by considering the dormouse, all rather odd in urban primary schools. This work was often conducted by pupils listening to a radio broadcast and reading an accompanying booklet, which suggests that at the time teachers needed support even in the teaching of nature study. Pedagogically, these lessons were closer to literacy lessons than to contemporary science lessons.

The Plowden Report (CACE 1967) made some reference to the teaching of science and suggested that it should become a feature of the curriculum. In the report, they made reference to having observed science but noted how unusual it was. It is clear, reading the report now, that the authors were encouraging schools to make science a major part of the curriculum. In the 1970s the Schools Council instigated a major curriculum project on the teaching of science; it is equally clear that few schools took that message. In the wake of Plowden, a Schools Council project *Science 5–13* was established to develop and disseminate good practice in the teaching of science in primary schools. Its first publication, *With Objectives in Mind: Guide to Science 5–13* (Ennever 1972) came out in 1972. The title of this first book in the series is instructive, in that it set an agenda for the way curriculum planners should think about science. For the first time, the project set out both the content and the teaching methods to be employed for the teaching of science. What the project workers did was to attempt to wed together a process-oriented mode of teaching with a behavioural objectives perspective. The project set out clearly what the overall objectives were to be. For the first time, it was proposed that primary school children should learn science and that science should cover more than nature study; rather, biology, physics and some aspects of chemistry should also be included. Arguably this project was the progenitor of National Curriculum Science. In the case of the National Curriculum, the programme is set out under the following headings. You will be familiar with these attainment targets from the 2000 curriculum document:

Sc1 Scientific enquiry
Sc2 Life processes and living things
Sc3 Materials and their properties
Sc4 Physical processes.

The emphasis that the National Curriculum puts on enquiry should make science an ideal subject for the development of the kind of pedagogy that we are writing about. Proper enquiry requires action and exploration, but it needs more than that; it needs purposeful talk. Through speech, pupils can make their meanings clearer and can begin to explicate some of the complex abstract concepts used in science. Have you seen this in the classrooms you have worked in?

What you will be familiar with is the content of the science curriculum. While 'life processes and living things' have some relationship to the old topic of nature study, the curriculum actually introduces biology – including human biology. Sc3 and Sc4 are very different from anything that was taught on a regular basis before the advent of the National Curriculum.

Science 5–13 was also important and influential in the way it described how science was to be taught. The pedagogy it proposed was firmly based in Piagetian theory. What was stressed was the child as an investigator. Science was to be learnt by getting the children to engage in purposeful activities. But it went beyond this, in that it proposed that the children should not be given the 'answers' but should discover the 'facts' of science through observation, experimentation and investigation. What was being argued was a move away from simple direct instruction towards individual and group work. It was assumed that primary classrooms would be organised in such a way that more than one subject would be covered in any given time, and thus the idea of a science investigation group working at task without supervision was recommended.

Activity

Thus science with five- to thirteen-year-olds might best be described as a means of structuring opportunities for a child to have scientific 'experiences' within his environment. From well ordered observation would come questions, leading towards investigations and the need for systematic means of recording what has been found out. A case can be made for the facts encountered, whilst of value in themselves, being less important than the child's adoption of a problem solving approach. (Schools Council 1980: 7)

Compare the way that *Science 5–13* describes the nature of science for the age group to what the National Curriculum has to say. Also compare the content set out in, for instance, 'Mini Beasts 1 and 2' and 'Structures and Forces Stages 1 and 2' with the comparable programmes of study in the National Curriculum.

If you analyse the way that National Curriculum science is to be taught, you will find that it is very much underpinned by a Piagetian framework. Attainment target Sc1 makes great use of the verb 'to investigate' and the noun 'evidence'. It also talks about children learning through first-hand experience. The expected dialogic shift was to raising questions, and this idea of raising questions has been a constant theme of science educators seeking to improve the quality of learning in science. Wynne Harlen, one of the most distinguished science educators in the UK and a principal worker on the *Science 5–13* project, makes clear that it is children's questions not just teachers' questions that are important. She is saying (Harlen 1996) that we need to move beyond Piaget's notion of the child as an individual explorer/investigator and put the work of science in a social constructivist context. It is not just doing, but talking with others including the teacher, which should inform teachers' planning and implementation of science lessons.

The teacher may know the answers, so there is no point in withholding them. In the following example, the teacher knew where the bird's nest had come from and helped the children identify the 'stuff' as hair. But for the length of hatching, she did not have the knowledge and the conversation ran as follows:

T: Well you've asked me a question that I can't answer – how many days it would take – but there's a way that you could find out, do you know?

C: Watch it?

C: A book?

T: Yes, this something you could look up in a book and when you've found out …

C: (*who rushed to pick up the book by the display of the nest*) ... I've got one here somewhere.

C: Here, here's a page about them.

T: There we are.

Harlen herself goes on to say:

> Turning questions into investigable ones is an important skill since it enables teachers to treat difficult questions seriously but without providing answers beyond children's understanding. It also indicates to children that they can go a long way to finding answers through their own investigation, thus underlining the implicit messages about the nature of scientific activity and their ability to answer questions by 'asking the objects'.
>
> (Harlen 1996)

The attainment targets of the National Curriculum set out in detail the content that has to be covered. One result of the detail is that many teachers seem to be driven by a concern to cover the content rather than focusing on the process of scientific investigation described in Sc1, the kind of thing that Harlen argues for above. It has been reported that in a number of primary classrooms, the ratio of investigatory work to 'chalk and talk' method is very low. Ofsted reports on individual schools make this clear and the annual reports of the Chief Inspector have also commented on the tendency to underplay investigation and to teach didactically. It is probable that what is foremost in teachers' minds is the scores that pupils attain in the science SATs. We pointed out in earlier chapters that whole class teaching can engage with pupils in ways which are not didactic, that challenge them to think and to explore, and this can be done in science teaching, as we shall show.

It is a Wednesday afternoon and a Year 4 class are seated on the floor in the school hall. They have previously visited a university and investigated the nature of forces. Now the university lecturer reminds them of their work and sets the scene for the work of the afternoon. He uses a football to demonstrate. He rolls a football to a boy who kicks it.

T: What's he doing with his feet?

P: (*Unison.*) Kicking.

T: What else?

P: Outside.

T: OK, kicking with the outside of your foot. // He's pushing the ball with the outside of his foot. Erm erm, what do you call that?

P: Pull push, erm, force makes it move.

T: Yes, a force.

Basically the teacher is using carefully constructed questions to check that pupils have the knowledge he previously taught them. We might note that while the form is of questions of fact, he is very careful to draw out the scientific term 'force' from the children, not to supply it.

He then proceeds to get another boy to hold the ball in the air.

T: What will happen if he lets it go?
P: (*Unison.*) It falls.
PI: Erm gravity.
T: Well done, yes, the force called gravity. So why doesn't it fall?
PI: A force pushes up.

Unlike the teaching of mathematics and English, good science teaching has always been seen as requiring a set of practical activities through which the teacher supports investigatory actions. So this lesson continues with pupils being organised into working groups. In these groups, the pupils use inclined planes and wheeled vehicles made from Lego. The task of each group is to make three different vehicles and then to measure the distance they travel against the angle of the inclined plane.

Guest and Postlethwaite (2000) make clear the need for exploration and investigation:

> Teaching science to primary school age children is about providing experiences and helping children to structure those experiences. Sometimes children will need guidelines, direction or even detailed explanations. (Ibid.: 136)

The pupils proceed to make further exploration of the forces. They can do this because they have been provided with guidance and explanation that enables them to explore productively. The task is not simply to make something with Lego and let it roll down an inclined plane, but to make particular vehicles and – under controlled conditions – explore and measure how forces act on them. As the pupils work on the task, it becomes clear that they have internalised the particular words that denote the scientific concepts they are exploring. The pupils talk of measuring distance in centimetres, having rejected the metre as too large. They also discuss how the angle of inclination affects the acceleration of the vehicle and the distance it will travel. Two pupils use the term 'acceleration', although it was not introduced in this lesson. This shared use of technical language demonstrates a confident conceptual understanding and models the use of such language for their peers.

What we note in both the whole class teaching episode and the group work is the way in which the pupils and teachers stick very tightly to the learning objective for the lesson. The National Curriculum for science does not specify learning outcomes in the way that the national strategies specify them, but even so what we can observe is a tight and highly organised lesson. The consistent use of the phrase 'Pupils should be taught' focuses attention on what are learning outcomes, albeit that they are somewhat broader than *Science 5–13*'s objectives. We would argue that that is directly in the tradition of organising science originally proposed in *Science 5–13*. The use of 'technical scientific language' by the teacher and also by at least some of the pupils is a powerful indicator that this pedagogical stance has been accepted and is being used.

Activity

Draw up an observation schedule that will enable you to record the progress of pupils' work during science activities. Use the categories set out in Chapter 3 to help you.

What kind of interventions, if any, would you make when the pupils are working and why?

In earlier chapters we made reference to Bernstein's concept of classification. We would argue that, of the core subjects, science – like mathematics – is very strongly classified. In the episode alluded to above, you can see how the teacher says 'OK, kicking with the outside of your foot.// He's pushing the ball with the outside of his foot. Erm erm, what do you call that?' This question can have several answers. For example, it could be described as a 'pass' if it was classified by a football coach, but it is a science teacher and the pupil responds 'Pull push, erm, force makes it move'. The teacher confirms this is the correct response, 'Yes, a force'. So here, the knowledge is classified as science not sport. The work is also tightly framed. The framing comes about in the first instance from the opening whole class teaching session, when the teacher focuses the children not just on the concept of forces but also on the mode of investigation. You can also see how Harlen is arguing for tight framing in her discussion of investigable questions.

The lesson proceeds and the teacher puts examples of recording sheets on an overhead projector.

T: Now I've made this record sheet for you to follow. You put the measurement in this column, the distance in this one and the angle here. It's important to follow it.

The record sheet is a concrete model of the instructional discourse, which structures how the process of investigation will proceed.

We stated earlier that primary science now is very different in content and perhaps in practice to what was done in even in the recent past. Our example above you will recognise as elementary physics. The authors remember that, many years ago when they were at school, it was covered in the second year of secondary schooling, not at primary school. Our next example comes from what would traditionally be labelled as chemistry.

A group of primary pupils have come to the university to work in the special primary science rooms. It is an opportunity for them to work in groups supported by a trainee teacher. The pupils come into the room where the tasks are already set out on the tables, in rather the same manner that technicians set up experimental apparatus for undergraduates. Each group of four pupils is supported by a trainee. In this case, the university lecturer introduces the work not by stating what the task will be but by describing the apparatus and setting out simple health and safety rules.

T: Now here are some candles – er nightlights – and they're in sand so they can't fall over and burn you / and the board won't burn, so if you drop the match it's safe.

After this statement the children nod and the trainees point to the nightlights and boards.

T: Now we are going to make sort of spoons with this, erm, silver foil and you can hold it with these wooden clothes pegs. Why?
P: 'Cos metal conducts heat and wood doesn't.
T: Yes, well done. Did you hear? It means you won't burn yourself. Yeah, metal conducts heat and wood doesn't.

Although the teacher has been simply describing and instructing, he takes the opportunity to challenge the pupils with a cognitive question. Having got an answer, he takes up the pupil's idea and reformulates for the whole class.

Until the advent of the National Curriculum, chemistry was not something taught in primary schools. What this lesson shows is that primary school children can learn chemistry and come to some understanding of how chemical change comes about. We emphasised above that investigation is not simply giving pupils objects and telling them to discover something. In this case, the lesson has been planned with clear objectives and the apparatus carefully selected and presented. This does not mean that the children have to get the 'right' answer. The process of investigation, in this case, requires predictive observation and drawing judicious conclusions from available evidence. It is the process that is the main aim of this lesson, a process that is generalisable to other science activities. What the trainees are attempting to do as they work with the pupils is to create discourses around the themes and ideas of the way materials are changed through the process of heating, and this is more challenging than it seems. Meeting the first attainment target, Sc1 Scientific enquiry, requires pupils to be able to discuss and give oral recounts.

The focus of the investigation is the nature of change – in this case, a consideration of permanent change. The advantages of having trainees with each group become obvious from the beginning of the lesson. Trainees are able to initiate discussion about the substances that will be heated and, as the process proceeds, move the discussion onwards. The dialogue in one group of four pupils and a trainee is representative. After the whole class introduction, the teacher trainee (TT) demonstrates how to make a 'spoon' out of foil and gives a running commentary as she does so. The pupils' (P) attention is focused on the apparatus and the substances they will heat and the language is descriptive and predictive.

TT: What substances do you think we've got?
P: Erm, chocolate.
TT: Yes, chocolate and … (*no response*) flour, salt, sugar, raisins and those crystal things for cakes.

The trainee now moves into a direct instructional dialogue. Reminding the pupils of what they have to do – i.e. heat the substance – the trainee then focuses their attention on the investigation. This will require the pupils to observe carefully, but first to make predictions of what changes will occur.

TT: You take a little bit of the substance and heat it, then we watch what happens / What do you think?
P: It'll change colour.
TT: You think so?
P: Yeah and it'll go black at the end.
TT: OK, let's see. Watch carefully.
P2: Do we write it, Miss?
TT: Oh yes, good boy, on the record sheet.

What is happening is that the trainee is trying to set up a scientific discourse. She is supporting the pupils in their use of language as much as she is supporting them in the task. Look at how she responds to the statement that the substance will change colour. She doesn't agree but stresses that this is a pupil's own idea and this enables the pupil to extend his ideas. At the end of the extract, she accepts and takes on board what pupil 2 says about recording the investigation. Recording is a very important aspect of any scientific investigation, because it enables recount and reflection and, importantly, enables repeatability.

Here is an example of a teacher working with a group of four Year 4 pupils. He is setting up some empirical work (teaching science, Attainment 1, or AT1) but begins by exploring the pupils' knowledge and experience. The pupils and the teacher are seated around a large table. He will later ask them to predict and test. There is tray with five balls made of different substances, which are also different sizes.

T: Which ball is bounciest? What might you do?
P1: When you, er er, drop them?
T: Yes, right.
P2: Be careful of the marble.

T: Why would you be careful of the marble?

P2: It might smash.

T: It might smash.

P3: Delicate.

T: So you might drop them. What good is that going to do?

P3: Well.

P4: It'll bounce.

T: We'll see it bounce, yes.

P3: Well, it it cos of the force, it it might cos it's got a hard surface / it will bounce up.

T: Alright OK, so how are we going to do it? Shall er er, are you just going to drop them?

P4: Hold them all at the same height.

T: Hold them all at the same height.

The teacher's first utterance comprises two different but related questions. The first relates to knowledge (physics), the second to method. The pupils respond to the question as being solely about method. The issue raised about the marble is an operational one rather than one about the substance it is made of. But what we can note is the way the teacher takes up pupil 2's idea by repeating the utterance but ignores the interjection, 'delicate'. Although the teacher is seeking to ask questions of fact, he leaves the pupils the space to respond in their own way. At times he does not take up an idea, he accepts, for instance, the idea of a hard surface without looking for more explanation. His use of fillers shows him trying to come to terms with the pupils' thinking and, as the dialogue proceeds, we see pupils introducing the idea of fair testing, with 'Hold them all at the same height' being repeated by the teacher.

Here is an example we have taken from a book on primary science (Ollerenshaw and Ritchie). The children had been investigating snails, and they had been allowed to investigate what they thought was important about snails. Here we see the teacher checking what they have done.

T: What have you found out about snails?

P4: They're gooyey and cold.

P2: That's because they're slimy.

T: Why are they slimy?

P2: So that they can stick to things and climb walls. When it stops, it makes slime where it has been.

T: Where was the slime?

P3: On the carpet – a lot.

We see pupil 4 respond but then there is a little interaction with pupil 2, who offers another explanation and then goes on to explain the function of slime. You can see that the teacher accepted this and sought extension.

We have taken the following extract from a television programme whose aim is the professional development of teachers engaged in the delivery of science. It comes from a Channel 4 series entitled *Making Sense of Science* (Channel 4 TV 2001).

In the section we have extracted, a Year 2 class are shown seated on the carpet facing the teacher; she introduces the topic.

T: We are going to do some work with shadows today. / Before we start, could somebody tell me what a shadow is?

P: Sun, er, shines on it an' when the sun can't go through you, it makes a black patch by you.

T: By you, yes, where else can the shadow be, Jamie?

P: In front of you.

T: In front of you. When would it be in front of you?

P: When the sun is behind you.

T: When the sun is behind you, yes. Could it be anywhere else?

P: Beside.

T: Do shadows change during the day?

P: Shorter.

T: And when will the shadows be longer?

P: When the sun is low down, in the evening, the shadows are long.

Here we have a sequence of questions which draw on pupils' common knowledge and then lead them to a scientific description of shadows; this takes them from common sense to scientific knowledge. The first question seeks to establish what the pupils know about shadows – not in a common sense manner but in a scientific manner. The teacher is not simply seeking factual responses. As her questions proceed, we can see how the questions establish a cognitive structure for understanding the relationship between the length of shadows and the position of the sun. This skilful use of questions shows how the whole, not the parts, offer cognitive challenge and subsequently cognitively structure the pupils' knowledge.

Lessons to be learnt

We said earlier that primary science has now established a tradition of exploratory group activity. Having said that, reports by Ofsted and the comments of many local authority science advisors suggest that the tradition is not followed as universally as it might be. What we can see from the commentary above is that whole class teaching has an important role in science teaching. At the opening of the lessons, the teacher not only sets the task but also, by the careful use of cognitively challenging questions, sets an intellectual climate for the pupils. The movement from whole class organisation to small groups is and always has been challenging. What skilful teachers do, when they begin and usually end with the whole class, is to make the task to be done explicit and ensure that the pupils can identify that the group task is part of the whole lesson. Primary teachers have the advantage of having learning assistants (hereafter LAs) to work with. The number of these has increased and government policy means that their number will increase further in future years. Such assistants will be available to guide and support small groups, but they will need guidance in turn from the teacher in order to be able to scaffold rather than tell. The trainees we recorded show how valuable it is to have a trained adult in a group. In order for these adults to be effective, they need careful instruction. The teacher must now plan for the LA's role. This planning will aim to ensure that they use challenging questions and create discursive focused talk in small groups, rather than simply supporting and asking factual questions. This planning seeks to engage children and transform their common knowledge into scientific curriculum knowledge – an aim that can be supported by the work of Edwards and Mercer (1987).

Activity

Design and plan a science activity. Create a 'prompt' sheet for a learning supporter, or trainee or volunteer adult, which will show them how to scaffold the pupils' language use through the kinds of questions asked, the focus of the questions and the sequence of the questions.

Chapter 10

Responding to individual need in whole class teaching

In this chapter, you will see how teachers:

- keep a focus on pupils' learning in the context of rapid policy change, by offering
  - match
  - differentiation
  - personalised learning
- respond to pupils with additional needs
- deal with the challenge of teaching mixed-age classes
- create an inclusive classroom dialogue.

The challenge of meeting the entitlement of pupils who experience special educational needs is a perennial one for all teachers. Since the publication of the Warnock Report (HMSO 1978), schools and teachers have engaged in a struggle to establish a pedagogy that is inclusive while at the same time supporting the needs of those experiencing the most difficulties. It is in the teaching of mathematics and English that the most attention has been paid to special needs. Alongside this, considerable efforts have been put into promoting behaviour for learning. Perhaps equally challenging for primary school teachers is designing and implementing lessons in classes with mixed-age groups, and this occurs most often in small rural schools. The data we will draw on in this chapter reflect the way teachers meet both these challenges. These issues are not new, so before turning to our own data we will examine the key pedagogical concepts of 'match', 'differentiation' and 'personalised learning'.

Match

The Plowden Report (CACE 1967) emphasised the need for teachers to match curriculum and learning activities to the child's stage of development.

> The teacher's task is to provide an environment and opportunities which are sufficiently challenging for children and yet not so difficult as to be outside

their reach. There has to be the right mixture of the familiar and the novel, *the right match to the stage of learning the child has reached.* [our emphasis] (Ibid.: para 533, p. 196)

Any failure on the part of the teacher to do this leads to boredom and inattentiveness. What you can see is that the report does not focus on the child's chronological age but on a stage of development, thus children of around the same chronological age can be at very different stages of development. The problem of match is then not solved by dealing with an age group but by dealing with individuals to some greater or lesser degree. Harlen (Harlen *et al.* 1977) draws attention to the complexity of creating the kind of match proposed by Plowden, asking for instance how we can know what the 'realistic expectations of a child at different stages of development' are and how we can intervene with children who 'seem to make no progress'. In effect, this kind of match leads to individualisation and is virtually impossible to achieve in primary classes, because it requires sustained one-to-one interaction with the pupil. You will have noted how the strategies prioritise particular age groups over individuals.

The seminal Alexander, Rose and Woodhead report (Alexander *et al.* 1992) drew attention to the impossibility of individualisation and the need for teachers to plan for the teaching of whole classes, to develop whole class pedagogy. In saying this, they both simplify and reconceptualise the idea of 'match' by focusing attention on 'curriculum match'. Put simply, this involves the following:

- prioritising knowledge
- using a subject-based curriculum
- using logical sequencing of tasks
- covering the ground
- identifying the centrality of mismatch and repairing it.

Rather than seeking to match tasks to a stage of development, teachers are enjoined to identify when mismatch occurs and to repair it. In this model of match, which is mirrored so well by the strategies, the knowledge and tasks are aligned to age groups – that is, the stuff to be taught is divided into age-specific chunks. As you might have noticed, this way of teaching is now used in subjects other than English and mathematics, as we showed in the preceding chapters.

Activity

Go to www.teachernet.gov.uk and look at lesson plans under 'teaching and learning'. Select some for foundation subjects. Is the suggested organisation similar to that in the strategies? You will need to look carefully, as it may be implicit rather than explicit.

Hints
How often is the teacher expected to engage in whole class discussion?
When is it expected to take place during the lesson?
How much time is given over to beginnings and endings?

Another way of thinking about match is to consider it through the lens of social constructivism, a theme that runs through this book. In this case, it involves the following:

- prioritising classroom discourse
- drawing on Vygotskian ideas
- working in zones of proximal development
- valuing children's meaning-making activities.

This way of thinking about match refocuses it on the process of learning and how teaching is related to it. By identifying the children's zones of proximal development, the teacher is better able to select tasks that challenge the children but do not overwhelm them. And because meaning-making is prioritised, teachers do not have to create individual programmes of study.

Differentiation

Like 'match', 'differentiation' has a range of meanings, serving as a sort of useful cupboard in which a wide range of practices can be stored.

Her Majesty's Inspectors of Schools (HMI) suggest there are four broad strategies that teachers use to match work to differing pupils' abilities:

- outcome
- rate of progress
- enrichment
- setting different tasks (HMI 1992).

You may decide that the concept's range of convenience is so broad as to make it more or less meaningless. It has been part of educational jargon in England certainly since the late 1970s. HMI, as Pollard (1990) notes, introduced and then promoted the concept throughout the system:

> ... new concepts for the analysis of the curriculum gradually emerged, were legitimated by HMI (DES 1984), and began to pass into the language of the profession: progression, coherence, breadth, balance, differentiation. (Ibid.: 73)

HMI were very influential, in that they reported on the state of the system to the Secretary of State and organised courses for teachers focused on HMI concerns, wrote reports on education, and produced occasional publications aimed at describing and encouraging good practice. The idea of careful differentiation was identified as a key aspect of the good classroom practitioner; the list above identifies what should be done. In doing this, HMI produced a complex and at times almost contradictory account of differentiation. They saw differentiation by task as a requirement to meet the needs of the range of ability in all classes. Their pragmatic solution to the problem of individual differentiated tasks was to recommend group tasks, groups at times selected by ability. In the case of pupils identified as having special learning needs, the recommendation was for carefully individually differentiated tasks to meet the particular needs of the pupil. You will have encountered this form of differentiation in school, where you have met planning for children's individual needs. Another major way of talking about differentiation was to argue for the production of lesson planning that produced differentiated outcomes. Typically, teachers were encouraged to set more challenging assessment tasks for children, particularly those identified as gifted and talented. This HMI agenda is still evident in schools and can also be seen in the criteria for judgement used by Ofsted in its inspection of primary schools and teacher training establishments.

Perhaps the most common use of differentiation in the system is for pupils identified as having special educational needs, now often referred to as 'additional needs'. The Warnock Report (HMSO 1978) established the idea of special educational needs but described the majority of pupils with such as having 'transitory needs'; thus around 20 per cent of pupils were described as being likely to have a special need at some point in their school career, but only about 2 per cent were described as having ongoing special needs. When the Warnock Report argued for integration, it focused on differentiation as the way to integrate pupils with learning or other difficulties into the mainstream school. So for many schools and teachers, differentiation is taken to mean planning for those kinds of pupils. You will have seen this in schools you have worked in.

Activity

In your own plans and in school plans you have encountered, look for the word 'differentiation' and, under it, the terms 'core', 'support' and 'extension'. What is being planned here and for whom?

Again, if you look at the strategy documents you will see that differentiation is not a major theme; it comes in supplementary guidance. The key idea behind the strategies is that the children are taught as a whole class. This was at least partly inspired by observing teaching in the Pacific Rim, specifically Taiwan. Here children were observed being taught as a whole class and then progressing as a whole class; differentiation in this context was an alien concept. The *National Numeracy Strategy*, according to Whitburn (2000), had the intention of removing differentiated teaching. In England, the idea that the class progresses as a whole class is equally alien, since we still hold to some extent to the various ideas of differentiation that are discussed above. Teachers in England are still convinced that children learn at different rates and maybe in different ways, so the ideas of differentiation and match still have a professional resonance. No matter how hard policy-makers seek to change that professional orientation, it still stubbornly remains part of what teachers see as good classroom practice.

Personalised learning

The recent policy agenda on personalised learning can be seen as a response to the holding on to these ideas. What is being recommended is not always very clear; it is stated that personalisation is not individualisation nor does it appeal directly to the concepts of differentiation and match. The problem is what *is* meant by personalised learning or personalisation in the current context. Primary school teachers have become very accustomed to using the ideas of differentiation and match to create individual learning plans for pupils identified as having special educational needs. In a recent research report, Daniels and Porter (2007), commenting on the system as a whole, argue that a complex and at times confusing set of policies have impacted on teachers, pupils and classrooms. They note the steady increase in the number of pupils identified as having special educational needs in mainstream schools, and we have seen that the response to this at both classroom and national levels has been an attempt to deal with such pupils as individuals. This can be illustrated by the demands made to create Individual Education Plans (IEPs) during the late 1980s and the 1990s. What this meant was that, for certain aspects of the curriculum, particularly English and mathematics, work was differentiated to match the needs of individual pupils. You can see how this runs counter to the pedagogy of whole class teaching originally enshrined in the strategy documents, as Whitburn (2000) above states.

The central policy solution to the conundrum of identifying individual special educational needs in a regime dedicated to whole class teaching has been to focus attention on assessment for learning and the development of what is now called 'personalised learning'. This is defined, at least in an operational manner, in the five-year strategy statement (DfES 2004a). It was the view of the Secretary of State at the time that the creation of personalised learning must be in the context of the national strategies and whole class teaching and was a matter for teachers. This presents a considerable dilemma for teachers, particularly those accustomed to creating individual learning plans for pupils with some kind of special edu-cational need. It is likely that such teachers will be working in schools serving areas of economic and social deprivation. The achievement of pupils who learn in such schools and a focus on personalised learning as the way to enhance their achievement resonate with subsequent policy iterations (e.g. *The Children's Plan*, DfES 2007).

The Report of the Teaching and Learning in 2020 Review Group defined 'personalised learning' in the following way:

> Put simply, personalised learning and teaching means taking a highly structured and responsive approach to each child's and young person's learning, in order that all are able to progress, achieve and participate. It means strengthening the link between learning and teaching by engaging pupils – and their parents – as partners in learning.
>
> Personalised learning is not a new initiative. Many schools and teachers have tailored curriculum and teaching methods to meet the needs of children and young people with great success for many years. What is new is our drive to make the best practices universal across all schools, particularly for children whose needs can be the most challenging to meet. (DfES 2002)

You may find it difficult to see how this is any different from individualised learning plans, differentiated teaching or matching the curriculum to pupils' individual needs. We will now show how skillful teachers can maintain whole class pedagogies while also ensuring that all pupils, regardless of their aptitudes, capabilities and skills, can learn productively. You will have seen some evidence of this in our previous chapters. We will now look in some detail at how the classroom discourse of these teachers engages all pupils in learning through whole class interaction.

Responding to difference in whole class teaching

In previous chapters we showed you how, during literacy and mathematics teaching, our teachers sought to include all pupils. In order to do this, they had to keep in mind those pupils for whom learning was more challenging. In the Key Stage 1 literacy class (Chapter 5), the proportion of pupils identified as being in need was much higher than the national average and a higher proportion were entitled to free school meals, the latter being a recognised proxy for poverty. In the past, the expectation would have been that the most needy pupils would be removed from the lesson and, under their IEPs, receive specially tailored instruction. The advent of the strategies changed that and now all of the pupils are included in the mainstream classroom. This means that the teacher has to construct an inclusive instructional discourse, and you have seen a little of that in other chapters. Let us now look at some details.

In this class, a large number of learning outcomes were visited although the lesson focuses on six specific outcomes. At word level these were: discrimination of each phoneme, discriminating phonemes, securing phonemic spellings, reading on sight high-frequency words. At text level, the learning outcomes they worked on were making simple notes and using headings in non-fiction texts. In addition, they undertook sentence work on turning statements into questions. The teacher endeavored to keep all of the pupils in contact with the content but, in order to do this, she had to ensure that her questions on the learning outcomes were adjusted to each pupil she asked to speak. This tailoring of her nominations had the effect of enabling all pupils, including those experiencing the most difficulties, the maximum possibility of engaging with the learning outcomes. We can see from our analysis that although the pupils identified as having difficulties produced shorter utterances than others, they were prepared to respond and were sufficiently involved to volunteer responses when they were not nominated. Part of this skilled teacher's repertoire is to narrow the focus of the lesson for these pupils and, within the ebb and flow exchange, to provide them with the confidence to participate. Within this lesson the focus for these children is on the discrimination of each phoneme and then each syllable. At the same time, this teacher maintains a second strong focus for the whole class on turning statements into questions. The checking questions she uses ensure that the pupils with difficulties know what is going on. For all the pupils, the pedagogic discourse provides cognitive challenge. The effect of the discourse is that the pupils with difficulties engage and therefore require less contingency management and contest the teacher's authority less than the rest of the class.

We can now look in some detail at a similarly skilful use of pedagogy in a Key Stage 2 class. The focus of the lesson was on comparing informative and persuasive writing, visiting previous text-level work, previous word-level work and spelling rules for word endings. Once again, the teacher endeavours to keep all the pupils in contact with the content of the lesson and ensures they are involved in the process in an active manner. As was the case in the Key Stage 1 class, pupils identified as having difficulties normally produced shorter utterances than the others. In order to ensure that these pupils are part of the discourse the teacher, like his Key Stage 1 colleague, is prepared to narrow the focus – in this case, to comparing informative and persuasive writing and spelling rules. Again the teacher uses a range of checking questions to monitor the engagement with content of the lesson of all pupils. When doing this, he consistently addresses the pupils with difficulties, 'keeping them on board'. Another way in which he does this is to ask pupils with difficulties to draw on their common sense knowledge when discussing the text. What this teacher is doing is running a lesson within a lesson; this has the effect of presenting all pupils with cognitive challenge. The challenge is brought about by the teacher's pedagogical repertoire which we identify in the points below.

- The teachers readily nominated speakers and used nomination as means of including pupils with difficulties into the lesson.
- Given the nature of the literacy strategy, we are not surprised at the discrepancy in utterance and the number of utterances when we compare pupils with difficulties with all the rest.
- These teachers narrow the focus of the lesson and slow the pace of the learning for pupils with difficulties. They visit fewer learning outcomes with these pupils and do not introduce other learning outcomes into the mix. In brief,

they do not flip-flop from outcome to outcome, neither do they do this with the rest of the class.

- Where pupils take the content back, the teachers integrate that into the next episode of the lesson.
- They use a tighter selection of means of assistance with pupils with difficulties.
- We know that pupils with difficulties are engaged in these lessons because they are less likely to be subject to contingency management, they are not involved in issues of control and they volunteer individual responses to questions where there is no nominated speaker.

Activity
If you can, work with a partner to create a lesson script. In the script, show what kinds of questions you will use to create an inclusive discourse. Also make notes as to when, where and why you will narrow the focus and slow the pace.

If we look at a similar situation but this time consider the teaching of mathematics, we find that skilled teachers are able to reproduce the sort of pedagogy that includes pupils with difficulties. There is powerful anecdotal evidence that pupils with difficulties are more likely to be left reiterating past work or be left stranded and unable to follow the pattern and structure of a lesson introducing new knowledge. In the lessons we will now discuss, pupils with difficulties were all included but the teachers faced the challenge of dealing with two different year groups. This meant they had to deal with different content in the same lesson while keeping all the pupils engaged. Earlier we showed you how tightly organised were the mathematics lessons we studied. Teachers worked on one learning outcome at a time, creating an episodic structure for the lesson. In both age groups we found that our skilled teachers:

- work with the youngest learners first
- focus, when working with them, on one specific learning outcome at a time
- begin by asking cognitively challenging questions and rehearse pupil responses with other pupils
- check that they know that the youngest learners are following the content of the lesson. The questions do not exclude the older pupils, although older pupils are not normally nominated at this stage.
- engage with the older learners in the middle of the lesson. Again, they begin by asking cognitively challenging questions and then rehearse responses and use checking questions targeted on older pupils.
- enable older pupils to address content and mathematical questions in their own way

- engage, at the very end of the lesson, either the younger or older pupils in discursive questioning, before the pupils move on to individual or group work.

Here we see teachers managing a lesson within a lesson, adapting the content and pace of the lessons to the two age ranges whilst maintaining the engagement of all the pupils.

Earlier in this chapter, we drew your attention to the difference between differentiation and match and personalised learning as defined by central policymakers. We have hinted that there seems to be more similarity than difference. Throughout this book we have also made the point that individualisation is a chimera. It may be that the examples that we have sketched out above enable you to identify more clearly what personalised learning might look like. It seems to us, drawing on our examples, that to meet the criteria for personalisation within whole class teaching the following are necessary but probably not sufficient:

- running a lesson within a lesson
- narrowing the focus for target groups whilst keeping the interest of the whole class
- modifying the pace of lessons, slowing and speeding up the changes between learning outcomes in response to pupil utterances and substantive learning outcomes
- ensuring an inclusive pedagogic discourse such that no pupil is left outside the lesson. This important principle applies to issues of gender, linguistic diversity, cultural diversity and specific learning difficulties as well as those we have explicitly visited.

You should now go to the central government websites which seek to show what personalised learning is all about. It would also be useful for you to discuss this with teachers in school, to see whether the issues can be clarified.

In this chapter, we began with a discussion of key concepts employed, especially by HMI and by Ofsted, to describe good practice. We have offered a brief analysis of the concepts of match, differentiation and personalised learning. In doing that, we have suggested that in the format in which they are normally presented they lead to individualisation, which is impossible in practice and a contested idea.

We have summarised some key features of the work of our skilled teachers and, in doing so, have been able to describe how they teach classes with large groups of children with additional needs – emphasising the way they slow the pace and narrow the focus of teaching for this group, whilst maintaining overall pace and breadth of learning outcomes. We also described how they teach classes with two age ranges by carefully sequencing the way they assist learning and the content.

We have described versions of whole class teaching that are inclusive and meet the needs of all pupils and engage them all whilst targeting different groups at different times. We have shown how skilled teachers structure their lessons in a subtle manner, so that they do not ignore groups of pupils at given times. In so doing, we have introduced the idea of a lesson within a lesson.

Chapter 11

Remarks in conclusion

In this book, we have shown you a number of examples of teaching. We have also commented on them and tried to point out where we think that teachers are having a particular impact on the quality of children's learning. The teachers we have used as our sample are highly skilled and held in great respect. We can all learn from such colleagues, even if we don't quite meet their very high standards. It is important to learn how to become more effective by using the example of such skilled and experienced teachers. This does not mean simply copying what they do. It is essential to have a mode of analysis that enables you to identify the features that make up an effective pedagogy. In the book *Women Teaching Boys* (Ashley and Lee 2003), the authors report that what boys, and indeed all pupils, want is good and effective teaching.

The problem we all face is that there is no easy definition of 'effective teaching'. The literature on school effectivity has relied on identifying effectivity by the scores that students achieve on specified tests. The collection by Croll and Hastings (1996) makes it clear that effective teaching demands much more than this. For instance, we have focused on classroom talk and only in the background considered the organisation of the classroom and the way that teachers establish an ethos conducive to teaching and learning rather than simply implementing control. But assessment has become a high-stakes issue for schools, and the effectiveness movement has tried to find the correlates that indicate what kinds of things are more likely to lead to an effective school and effective teaching. This movement has focused on headship – on management and leadership – rather than on classroom practice. Originally Mortimore *et al.*'s (1988) study noted that better results were found in classrooms where, at maximum, two curriculum areas were dealt with. Subsequent to this pioneering study, it has become taken for granted that teachers should teach a single subject to whole classes. Policy in recent years has pushed a pedagogy that involves whole class teaching of single subjects, and that has been the focus of this book.

This book has focused on language use in the classroom. While changes in language use are not a simple and easy way to 'fix' problems of learning and teaching in contemporary primary schools, they are – as we have argued – crucial in creating a good environment conducive to learning. It is essential that teachers understand how language can be used to improve their teaching and consequently their pupils' learning. Coming to an understanding is no easy matter. It means we have to have knowledge of research methods and the results of research pertinent to the question of classroom language use. Sometimes this may seem obscure and overly difficult, but it is worth the effort. In the first part of this book, we took you through some studies of psychology and discourse analysis, and we did this so that you could gain the skills to reflect on your own practice in a scientific manner. Studies in both psychology and discourse analysis show how talk is used in classrooms but, more importantly, show us how we can use our own talk to better effect.

Recently, English primary education has come under a great deal of criticism. Alongside this, central government has become more and more confident in telling teachers what to do in their classrooms. We remarked earlier how, at the point of setting up the National Curriculum, the Secretary of State said it was improper to tell teachers how to teach – even though he was prescribing the content of lessons. Primary teachers are now being heavily advised or even instructed in how to teach the curriculum. Much of this advice or instruction comes from those convinced that they know the best way to improve achievement and that a key to it is setting targets. Unfortunately what many of these critical commentators ignore is the relationship between teaching and learning. It would be strange to claim that a lesson had been really well taught but pupils had learnt nothing. Sometimes commentaries on primary practice ignore what the pupils do and focus entirely on the teacher. Our examples show evidence of pupils learning because the teachers are eager to seize upon the pupils' ideas. We have offered you a way to analyse and describe what skilful teachers do with talk. It is worth noting that all of our examples come from teaching in challenging circumstances.

In Chapter 4 we discussed the way in which we collected data and also showed you our way of coding classroom talk. In the Appendix, we have put a coding sheet which we hope you will find useful in describing and analysing your own practice and perhaps that of your colleagues. It is the kind of coding sheet we have used ourselves, so we are able to say it is robust and fairly comprehensive. As you can see, it prompts you to be precise about language use and specific about both the number of utterances and the number of words per utterance. Without a robust and reliable way of describing what goes on in classrooms, it is not possible to analyse it and to draw the sorts of conclusions that say if we want to achieve more of 'x', then we should also be doing more of 'y'. So we can say that teachers who use discursive questions are more likely to hear their pupils making sustained, cognitive-oriented utterances, or to put it another way, they are encouraging pupils to think on their feet. We hope you will have noted that the code framework we described can be applied to all teaching in the primary school; it is not subject specific. Indeed one of the things you may have noticed is that it helped us to identify some specific differences in teaching that can be associated with the subject focus of the lesson.

In one of the cases we have shown you, can see a teacher working with a class with a very high percentage of pupils on the special educational needs register. Look back at how that teacher manages to include such pupils in the process of the literacy lesson. In your own teaching, you might want to identify in your plans when and who you want to nominate to respond to questions and to comment on significant ideas. Sheila was encouraging these young pupils, many with learning difficulties, to enter a process that became discursive; they are learning what a dialogic classroom will be like.

Our record of mathematics lessons shows that effective teachers are able not just to keep objectives in mind but deliberately to visit one learning outcome at a time. This is important for all pupils, but is particularly when teachers are dealing with a mixed-age range. The way the content of mathematics is described in the documents makes it sequential, so the challenge for the teacher is dealing with learning outcomes which essentially follow each other. The teacher we have focused on has lessons not just for mixed-age classes but also for classes in which the differences in learning capacity between students is very great. She is able to provide for those pupils by careful instruction and questioning. If you look back at what she does, you might consider how you can incorporate it into your own planning.

Teaching and learning are very complex human activities. We make no apology for focusing on teaching in this book, but in doing so we have tried to show how learning relates to teaching. Good teachers are always trying to scaffold pupils' knowledge and thus to enhance their understanding. Teacher talk is not merely conversation. It is the nuts and bolts of the job. It is how we assemble learning and strive to make it visible to the pupils. Talk is the vehicle by which knowledge is spread around the classroom. Our analysis has explored this phenomenon.

The analysis enables us to identify the kinds of language use that promote better learning. Effective teachers are very good at using the kinds of questions that enable them to check their pupils' factual knowledge. Aligned with this is getting the pupils to recall previous learning. Although these questions may seem trivial, they are an important device in teaching. They become less powerful, oddly enough, if they are overused. Overuse of 'Guess what teacher's thinking?' or 'What does the pupil know?' questions is unlikely to enhance pupils' learning. Our teachers were rapid in their use of these forms of questions and deliberately nominated pupils to respond. Often in doing this they made sure they were visiting only one learning outcome or made explicit to the pupils what the theme was. This nomination created an inclusive classroom environment. What they are doing is differentiating the pace of the lesson in terms of learning outcomes and utterance length. In brief, these teachers know when to slow down in order to change the kinds of questions they are using.

What is it about the language use of skilled teachers that we are recommending to you? Most of us are good at the kinds questions mentioned above, but in order to enhance learning we need much more sophisticated language use. The key is to use the outcomes of an assessment question to develop thinking through discursive language use. We identify four aspects to this. The first aspect is asking pupils what they think or feel. This is no easy matter and, as we argued in Part One, most studies of classroom interactions and exchanges show very little of this kind of language use. The second aspect is asking pupils to clarify the meanings they have made. The third aspect is drawing on common classroom knowledge and finally, the fourth is changing the direction of talk to incorporate the pupils' ideas and opinions. What this means is that the teacher validates pupils' ideas and then uses them in subsequent questioning and discussion. It takes both skill and confidence to do these kinds of things. The analytic framework we have provided enables you to identify when and where you are using language in this way; this will in turn help you to plan lessons such that discursive language use is maximised.

It is commonplace to say that language and thought are bound together. Good teachers model how to organise ideas and they do this through their use of language. They also prompt pupils to use language in such a way that they make their thinking clearer to themselves and to other pupils. Teachers who do this well recognise that hesitations, repetitions and fillers are signs of productive thinking, not things to be eradicated from pupil talk. What is recognised is that the closer classroom language can be brought to ordinary language use, the better the opportunities for learning will be. In short, a focus on learning means that pupils are entitled to the time that thinking takes and the time to express that thinking.

It may seem that we have sketched a single way to use talk in all classrooms. This is not really the case – there are general principles that can be applied, but when we look in detail at different subjects we can see differences. For instance, in the case of mathematics we can see a tight focus on a very limited number of learning outcomes dealt with one at a time, as we said above. In these lessons, virtually all the talk of both pupils and teachers is on task. English is different, although the talk is very much on task, because more learning outcomes are dealt with. We might expect that, since it is harder to separate English's learning outcomes one from another. The teacher may be focusing on reading and interpreting a text, but in the act of reading the pupil will visit a number of allied learning outcomes and the observant teacher will probably comment on them. Religious education provides an interesting example which, in our sample, contrasts with other subjects. Our examples of dealing with puzzling questions show that the discourse is more open ended and the pupils are prepared to speak freely about often contentious issues.

The focus of the book has been on whole class teaching. But as you can see in the case of science, this does not mean that teachers do not use group work. What they do is clearly establish the procedures by which groups will work and also the outcomes of this activity. The language they use is a model of how the pupils should use language in their group discussions. This does not mean that the pupils are expected to get the same answer, but that they will proceed to investigate in an appropriate manner. Alexander (2000) makes the point that the way that group work is set up and managed is critical to the way that pupils experience pace. The teachers to whom we have introduced you, by their use of language and the organisation of their classrooms, try to make their pedagogy visible – particularly to those pupils who may need additional support to make the most of their learning. What these teachers do is use talk in a discursive manner; they are happy to draw upon pupils' own cultural knowledge, viewing pupils as thinkers and thus enabling them to develop the cultural capital of formal school learning. In doing this, they include all pupils by the way they distribute school knowledge.

In the last chapter, we discussed how the pupils' experience of the lesson differed from the teacher's, in that the teacher often taught a number of lessons at the same time. The lesson targeted on pupils with special educational needs was not the same as that for others in the class – in Bernstein's terminology, it had a different 'framing'. We said that the teacher narrowed the focus to a particular set or individual learning outcome. The teacher selects the knowledge to be taught, and the sequence and speed (pace) at which learning outcomes are visited. Other pupils are engaged in talk about a more extensive range of leaning outcomes; they move through them more fluidly and thus pace for them is different. In the core curriculum, classification is always strong. We previously offered you a gloss on this important but difficult concept as the thing(s) that will be talked about and learnt, and defined framing as the order and sequence in which knowledge will be taught.

The talk of the teachers we have discussed can be characterised by the forms of utterance they employ and the way they deploy them in relation to subject knowledges. This produces a particular kind of classification and framing in which the classification remains strong but the framing enables pupils more easy entry into this formal knowledge. For example, our skilled teachers appeal to pupils to use their everyday knowledge to help them talk about important school knowledge. You will have noticed this in all our discussion of the teaching we have analysed. In a nutshell, skilled teachers ask the pupils to clarify what is being learnt and are willing to take the risk of following the pupils' direction even under the pressure to deliver specified content in specified time. They do not 'park' the learners' understandings in order to pursue their own. The idea of *Excellence and Enjoyment* (DfES 2003) to some extent sanctions this approach and offers teachers the opportunity to engage wholeheartedly in learning discourses with their pupils. Our data and data gathered by other researchers indicate that this kind of talk, this pedagogy, is enabling to the most disadvantaged pupils.

We are arguing that what is important is to use language in such a way that pupils are encouraged and enabled to express their own ideas. Questioning is not about checking their factual knowledge but about enabling them to think. The process of teaching is not just about instruction but about the development of thought. Pupils who have had modelled the kind of discursive language use we show in our examples are more likely to become confident learners and creative thinkers.

What we have tried to show you is that there are some general principles which underpin an effective primary pedagogy. But, as you will have noticed, this does not mean that teachers talk with their pupils in the same way all the time. Instead, they tailor their teaching to meet the variety of pupil audiences in their classrooms.

This is important in maintaining an inclusive learning environment, particularly for pupils likely to experience difficulties. You will also have noticed that effective teachers vary both their talk and the pupil talk they seek to promote with the kind of subject content they are focusing on. They do this within lessons and, more markedly, in different subject areas. So although there is a general pedagogy, these teachers are confident to vary this with audience and topic.

The current situation in English primary schools is one in which teachers are encouraged to be creative while they are subject to a myriad of central policy directives. We remarked earlier how, at the parliamentary debate on the National Curriculum, the then Secretary of State declared that ways of teaching – pedagogy – could only be a matter for teachers. Since that time, teachers have been bombarded with strong advice and directives as to how to teach. In the case of the *Literacy Strategy* and *Numeracy Strategy*, and now the *Primary National Strategy*, these policy directives reach directly into the classroom, trying to impose the way that teachers and pupils interact. It is important that teachers are able to analyse what is being demanded and to establish the business of teaching for themselves. There are many ways in which education policy has been analysed and critiqued; what we would argue is that, alongside those, you need to critically reflect on your own and on others' practices in the context of policy demands.

In this chapter, we have tried to provide an overview of the detailed analysis and description that runs through this book. We have endeavored to show you what an inclusive approach to classroom talk looks like and to illustrate this in a range of classroom contexts. We have argued that the ability to analyse the specifics of teaching and learning in all curriculum subjects enables us to understand how teachers' talk can make a positive difference to what all pupils learn. In so doing, we have returned to the work of Basil Bernstein. We have also suggested that the very same approach that enables teachers to critique policy directives enables them to protect the interests of their pupils and enhances their professional purchase on teaching and learning.

We hope that this book has made you more curious about the way that teaching and learning can be viewed and how they can become more effective. If you want to know more about the analysis behind our descriptions, you can find it in the following places: Eke *et al.* (2005) on religious education, and Lee and Eke (2004) on the teaching of literacy. Other writers you might find interesting are Mroz *et al.* (2000) on literacy, and Hancock and Mansfield (2002) on literacy and listening to children.

Appendix

Coding Sheet

Analysing classroom talk: utterance analysis

Transcript								
Line number at start of utterance				Actual number of words				
Word count	1–3	4–5	6–10	11–15	16–20	21–30	31–40	40+

Curriculum Content

Subject		Speaker
Learning outcome		Teacher
		Pupil: Girl Boy Unison
		Classroom Assistant

Assisted Performance	✓	Discursive features	✓
Modelling psycho-motor performance		WDPK1	
Modelling cognitive performance		WDPK2	
Assisting questions		GWTT1	
Assessment questions		GWTT2	
Feedback		D1 Discursive: clarification	

Assisted Performance	✓	Discursive features	✓
Instructions		D2 Discursive: what pupils think or feel	
Contingency management		Uptake	
Cognitive structuring: structures of explanation		Issues of power	
Cognitive structuring: structures of cognitive activity		Evidence of cognition	
Common classroom knowledge		Illocutionary take up	
Nomination of the speaker		Acknowledging pupils	
Speaker nominated Teacher Pupil: Girl Boy Unison Classroom Assistant			
Nominated Speaker responds			
Unison/Individual reading/counting			
Cultural knowledge			

Notes
Additional comments: For example: inaudible, laughter, learning transparency to the learner

Bibliography

Adams, M. J. (1990) *Beginning to Read: Thinking and Learning about Print* (Cambridge, Mass., MIT Press).

Alexander, R. (1992) *Policy and Practice in Primary Education* (London, Routledge).

Alexander, R. (2000) *Culture and Pedagogy: International Comparisons in Primary Education* (Oxford, Blackwell Publishing).

Alexander, R. (2004) *Towards Dialogic Teaching: Rethinking Classroom Talk* (2nd edn) (Cambridge, Dialogos).

Alexander, R., Rose, J. and Woodhead, C. (1992) *Curriculum Organisation and Classroom Practice in Primary Schools: A Discussion Paper* (London, DES).

Ashley, M. and Lee, J. (2003) *Women Teaching Boys: Caring and Working in the Primary School* (Stoke on Trent, Trentham Books).

Bakhtin, M. M. (1981) *The Dialogic Imagination* (Austin, University of Texas Press).

Barnes, D. (1977) *Communication and Learning in Small Groups* (London, Routledge and Kegan Paul).

Barnes, D., Britton, J. and Torbe, M. (1986) *Language, the Learner and the School* (Harmondsworth, Penguin Books).

Bennett, N. (1976) *Teaching Styles and Pupil Progress* (London, Open Books).

Bernstein, B. (1970) 'Education Cannot Compensate for Society', *New Society* 26 February, 1970, 344–7.

Bernstein, B. (1977) *Class, Codes and Control Vol. 3: Towards a Theory of Educational Transmissions* (rev. edn) (London, Routledge).

Bernstein, B. (1990) *Class, Codes and Control Vol. IV: The Structuring of Pedagogic Discourse* (London, Routledge).

British Telecom (2004) *The Digital Divide in 2005: An Independent Study Conducted for BT* (London, British Telecom).

Britton, James (1967) *Language and Learning* (Harmondsworth, Penguin).

Bruner, J. (1986) *Actual Minds, Possible Worlds* (Cambrige, Mass., Harvard University Press).

Burningham, J. (1984) *Granpa* (London, Cape).

Cazden, C. B. (2000) 'An Application of Basil Bernstein's Constructs of "Visible and Invisible Pedagogies"', in Power, S., Aggleton, P., Brannen, J., Brown, A., Chisholm, L. and Mace, J. *A Tribute to Basil Bernstein 1924–2000* (London, University of London, Institute of Education).

Central Advisory Council for Education (England) (CACE) (1967) *Children and Their Primary Schools* (Plowden Report) (London, HMSO).

Chall, J. (1970) *Learning to Read: The Great Debate* (New York, McGraw-Hill).

Croll, Paul and Hastings, Nigel (1996) *Effective Primary Teaching: Research-based Classroom Strategies* (London, David Fulton).

Croll, P. and Moses, D. (2000) *Special Needs in the Primary School: One in Five?* (London, Cassell).

Daniels, H. and Porter, J. (2007) 'Learning and Difficulties Among Children of Primary School Age: Definition, Identification, Provision and Issues', Primary Review Research Survey 5/2, (Cambridge, University of Cambridge, Faculty of Education).

Department for Education and Employment (DfEE) (1997) *National Literacy Strategy Framework for Teaching* (London, DfEE).

Department for Education and Employment (DfEE) (1999) *The National Numeracy Strategy* (London, DfEE).

Department for Education and Skills (DES) (1984) *The Curriculum 5–16: Curriculum Matters 2* (London, DES).

Department for Education and Skills (DES) (1985) *Education for All* (The Swann Report) (London, HMSO).

Department for Education and Skills (DES) (1989) *The National Handbook for Primary School Teachers* (London, DES).

Department for Education and Skills (DfES) (2002) 'Report of the Teaching and Learning in 2020 Review Group', http://publications.teachernet.gov.uk/eOrderingDownload/6856-DfES-Teaching%20and%20Learning.pdf.

Department for Education and Skills (DfES) (2003) *Excellence and Enjoyment: A Strategy for Primary Schools* (Nottingham, DfES).

Department for Education and Skills (DfES) (2004) *Learning and Teaching using ICT* (London, DfES).

Department for Education and Skills (DfES) (2004a) *Five Year Strategy for Children and Learners* (London, HMSO) Cmd 6272.

Department for Education and Skills (DfES) (2004b) *Primary National Strategy Learning and Teaching Using ICT* (CD ROM).

Department for Education and Skills (DfES) (2006) *Primary Framework for Literacy and Mathematics* (Nottingham, DfES).

Department for Education and Skills (DfES) (2007) *The Children's Plan* (London, DfES).

Earl, L., Watson, N., Levin, B., Leithwood, K., Fullan, M. and Torrance, N. with Jantzi, D., Mascall, B. and Volante, L. (2003) *Watching and Learning 3 Final Report of the External Evaluation of the Implementation of the National Literacy and Numeracy Strategies* (London, DfES)

Edwards, A. D. (1987) 'Language Codes and Classroom Practice', *Oxford Review of Education*, Vol. 13, No. 3: 237–47.

Edwards, D. and Mercer, N. (1987) *Common Knowledge: The Development of Understanding in the Classroom* (London, Routledge).

Eke, R. and Lee, J. (1991) 'Learning to be Legible: Children's Experience in a Lower Junior Classroom', *Primary Teaching Studies*, Vol. 6, No. 1.

Eke, R., Lee, J. and Clough, N. (2005) 'Whole-class Interactive Teaching and Learning in Religious Education: Transcripts from Four Primary Classrooms', *British Journal of Religious Education*, Vol. 27, No. 2, March 2005: 159–72.

English, E., Hargreaves, L. and Hislam, H. (2002) 'Pedagogical Dilemmas in the National Literacy Strategy: Primary Teachers' Perceptions, Reflections and Classroom Behavior', *Cambridge Journal of Education*, Vol. 32, No. 1: 9–26.

Ennever, L. (1972) *With Objectives in Mind: Guide to Science 5–13* (London, MacDonald Educational Press).

Galton, M. (1995) *Crisis in the Primary Classroom* (London, David Fulton Publishers).

Galton, M. and Simon, B. (eds) (1980) *Progress and Performance in the Primary Classroom* (London, Routledge and Kegan Paul).

Galton, M., Simon, B. and Croll, P. (1980) *Inside the Primary Classroom* (London, Routledge and Kegan Paul).

Galton, M., Hargreaves, L., Comber, C., Wall, D. with Pell, A. (1999) *Inside the Primary Classroom 20 Years On* (London, Routledge).

Goldman, R. (1965) *Readiness for Religion: a basis for developmental religious education* (London, Routledge and Kegan Paul)

Goswami, U. and Bryant, P. (1990) *Phonological Skills and Learning to Read* (Hove, Lawrence Erlbaum Associates).

Guest, G. and Postlethwaite, K. (2000) 'Development of the Science Curriculum' in Ashcroft, K. and Lee, J. (eds) *Improving Teaching and Learning in the Core Curriculum* (London, Falmer Press).

Halliday, M. (1975) *Learning How to Mean* (London, Edward Arnold).

Hancock, R. and Mansfield, M. (2002) 'The Literacy Hour: A Case for Listening to Children', *The Curriculum Journal*, Vol. 13, No. 2: 183–200.

Harlen, W., Darwin, A. and Murphy, M. (1977) *Match and Mismatch: Asking Questions* (Edinburgh, Oliver and Boyd).

Harlen, W. (1996) *The Teaching of Science in Primary Schools* (2nd edn) (London, David Fulton).

Haviland, J. (1988) *Take Care, Mr Baker* (London, Fourth Estate).

Hay, D., Nye, R. and Murphy, R. (1996) 'Thinking about Childhood Spirituality' in Francis, L. *et al.* (eds) *Research in Religious Education* (Leominster, Gracewing).

Her Majesty's Inspectorate (HMI) (1992) *Assessment Recording and Reporting: a report by HMI on the second year 1990–1991* (London, HMSO).

Her Majesty's Stationery Office (HMSO) (1978) *Special Educational Needs: Report of the Committee of Enquiry into the Education of Handicapped Children and Young People* (Warnock Report) (London, HMSO).

Hodge, R. and Tripp, D. (1986) *Children and Television* (Cambridge, Policy Press).

Lee, J. and Eke, R. (2004) 'The National Literacy Strategy and Pupils with Special Educational Needs', *Journal of Research in Special Educational Needs* Vol. 4, No. 1: 50–7.

Lewis, O. (1975) *Five Families: Mexican Case Studies in the Culture of Poverty* (New York, Condor).

Loach, K. (1988) *Kes* (film).

Lorac, C. and Weiss, M. (1981) *Communication and Social Skills* (Exeter, Wheaton).

Marsh, L. (1970) *Alongside the Child in the Primary School* (London, A. & C. Black).

Marshall, S. (1966) *An Experiment in Education* (Cambridge, Cambridge University Press).

McLure, J. (1992) 'The First Five Years' in Norman, K. (ed.) *Thinking Voices: The Work of the National Oracy Project* (London, Hodder and Stoughton).

Mercer, N. (1992) *Teacher Talk and Learning about the Media* in Alverado, M. and Boyd-Barret, O. (eds) *Media Education: An Introduction* (London, British Film Institute).

Mercer, N. (1995) *The Guided Construction of Knowledge: Talk Amongst Teachers and Learners* (Clevedon, Multilingual Matters).

Mercer, N. (2000) *Words and Minds: How We Use Language to Think Together* (London, Routledge).

Mercer, N. (2003) 'The Educational Value of "Dialogic Talk" in Whole Class Dialogues in QCA', *New Perspectives on Spoken English* (London, Qualifications and Curriculum Authority).

Mortimore, P., Sammons, P., Stoll, L., Lewis, D. and Ecob, R. (1988) *School Matters: The Junior Years* (Wells, Open Books).

Moyles, J., Hargreaves, L., Merry, R., Paterson, F. and Esarte-Sarries, V. (2003) *Interactive Teaching in the Primary School* (Maidenhead, Open University Press).

Mroz, M., Smith, F. and Hardman, F. (2000) 'The Discourse of the Literacy Hour', *Cambridge Journal of Education*, Vol. 30, No. 3.

Myhill, D., Jones, S. and Hopper, R. (2006) *Talking, Listening and Learning: Effective Talk in the Primary Classroom* (Maidenhead, Open University Press).

Nystrand, M., Gamoran, A., Kachur, R. and Prendergast, C. (1997) *Opening Dialogues: Understanding the Dynamics of Teaching and Learning in English Classrooms* (New York, Teachers College Press).

Ofsted (2002) *The National Literacy Strategy: The First Four Years 1998–2002*, HMI (555) (London, Ofsted).

Ofsted (2005) *Annual Report of Her Majesty's Chief Inspector of Schools 2004–2005* (London, Ofsted).

Ollerenshaw, C. and Ritchie, R. (1997) *Primary Science: making it work* (2nd edn) (London, David Fulton).

Organisation for Economic Cooperation and Development (OECD) (1995) *Measuring What Students Learn* (Paris, OECD).

Pogrow, S. (1998) 'What is an Exemplary Program, and Why Should Anyone Care? A Reaction to Slavin and Klein', *Educational Researcher*, Vol. 27, No. 7: 22–9.

Pollard, A. (1985) *The Social World of the Primary School* (London, Holt, Rinehart and Winston).

Pollard, A. (1990) *Learning in Primary Schools: An Introduction for Parents, Governors and Teachers* (London, Cassell).

Qualifications and Curriculum Authority (QCA) (1994) *Model Syllabus for Religious Education 1: Living Faiths Today* (London, QCA).

Qualifications and Curriculum Authority (QCA) (1994) *Model Syllabus for Religious Education 2: Questions and Teachings* (London, QCA).

Qualifications and Curriculum Authority (QCA) (2003) *Speaking Listening and Learning Key Stages 1 and 2 Handbook* (London, QCA).

Qualifications and Curriculum Authority (QCA) (2004) *Religious Education: The Non-statutory National Framework* (London, QCA).

Raiker, A. (2002) 'Spoken Language and Mathematics', *Cambridge Journal of Education*, Vol. 32, No. 1.

Raine, C. (1979) 'A Martian Sends a Postcard Home' (Oxford, Oxford University Press).

Reynolds, D. and Farrell, S. (1996) *Worlds Apart? A Review of International Surveys of Educational Achievement Involving England* (London, HMSO).

Riley, J. (2001) 'The National Literacy Strategy: Success with Literacy for All?', *The Curriculum Journal*, Vol. 12, No. 1: 29–52.

Rose, S., Lewontin, R. C. and Kamin, L. J. (1990) *Not in Our Genes: Biology, Ideology and Human Nature* (Harmondsworth, Penguin).

Rosen, C. (1971) 'Words and a World', in Jones, A. and Mulford, J. *Children Using Language* (Oxford, Oxford University Press).

Rosen, C. and Rosen, H. (1971) *The Language of Primary School Children* (Harmondsworth, Penguin).

Rosen, H. (ed.) (1975) *Language and Literacy in Our Schools* (London, University of London, Institute of Education).

Sharp, R. and Green, A. (1975) *Education and Social Control: A Study in Progressive Primary Education* (London, Routledge and Kegan Paul).

Simon, B. (1981) 'Why No Pedagogy in England?', in Simon, B. and Taylor, W. (eds) *Education in the Eighties, The Essential Issues* (London, Batsford).

Sinclair, J. McH. and Coultard, R. M. (1975) *Towards and Analysis of Discourse: The English Used by Teachers and Pupils* (Oxford, Oxford University Press).

Smith, F. and Hardman, F. (2003) 'Using Computerized Observation as a Tool for Capturing Classroom Interaction', *Education Studies*, Vol. 29, No. 1: 39–48.

Smith, F., Hardman, F., Wall, K. and Mroz, M. (2004) 'Interactive Whole Class Teaching in the National Literacy and Numeracy Strategies', *British Educational Research Journal*, Vol. 30, No. 3: 395–411.

Stigler, J. W. and Hiebert, J. (1997) 'Understanding and Improving Classroom Mathematics Instruction: An Overview of the TIMMS Video Study', *Phi Delta Kappan*, September: 14–21.

Tharp, R. and Gallimore, R. (1988) *Rousing Minds to Life: Teaching, Learning and Schooling in Social Contexts* (New York, Cambridge University Press).

Training and Development Agency (TDA) (2002) *Standards for Qualified Teacher Status* (London, TDA).

Varley, S. (1984) *Badger's Parting Gifts* (London, Andersen Press).

Vygotsky, L. (1978) *Mind in Society* (Cambridge, Mass., Harvard University Press).

Vygotsky, L. (1986) *Thought and Language* (Cambridge, Mass., MIT Press).

Wearmonth, J. and Soler, J. (2001) 'How Inclusive Is the Literacy Hour?', *British Journal of Special Education*, Vol. 28, No. 3: 113–19.

Wells, G. (1981) *Learning Through Interaction: The Study of Language Development* (Cambridge, Cambridge University Press).

Wells, G. (1987) *The Meaning Makers: Children Learning Language and Using Language to Learn* (London, Hodder and Stoughton).

Whitburn, J. (2000) *Strength in Numbers: learning maths in Japan and England* (London, National Institute of Economic and Social Research).

White, E. B. (1981) *Charlotte's Web* (London, MacMillan).

Wood, D. (1988) *How Children Think and Learn: The Social Contexts of Cognitive Development* (Oxford, Blackwell).

Young, R. (1992) *Critical Theory and Classroom Talk* (Clevedon, Multilingual Matters).

Young, R. (2002) 'Basil Bernstein's Sociolinguistic Theory of Language Codes', http://zimmer.csufresno.edu/~johnca/spch100/3-3-bernstein.htm.

Index